Mergers in Perspective
Yale Brozen

American Enterprise Institute for Public Policy Research
Washington and London

Yale Brozen is a professor of business economics in the Graduate School of Business at the University of Chicago, director of its applied economics program, and an adjunct scholar of the American Enterprise Institute.

I am grateful to Ernest Gellhorn and Donald G. Kempf, Jr., for their critical reading of the manuscript and their many suggestions. I, of course, am responsible for any remaining errors.

Y.B.

Library of Congress Cataloging in Publication Data

Brozen, Yale, 1917–
    Mergers in perspective.

    (AEI studies ; 353)
    1. Industrial concentration—United States—History.
2. Consolidation and merger of corporations—United States—History.   3. Industry and state—United States—History.   I. Title.   II. Series.
HD2795.B835   338.8′3′0973   82–3937
ISBN 0–8447–3489–6
ISBN 0–8447–3483–7 (pbk.)   AACR2

AEI Studies 353

Printed in the United States of America

Contents

Tables

Figures

1
Introduction

The United States has the world's most stringent merger laws. While policy in most other countries has aimed at encouraging mergers or has been neutral, that in the United States has been manifestly hostile to this activity.[1]

The chief difference in the design of domestic and foreign merger policy is the lively sense displayed abroad of the economic gains that size confers. Europe's post–World War II economic policies, for example, deliberately aim at producing an economic structure comparable to that of the United States. In particular, the European Economic Community (EEC) was intended to provide a market large enough to support firms as big as those in the United States. "The EEC's industrial policy is to encourage size," writes *The Economist*, Britain's prestigious weekly.[2] The policies followed in individual countries are consistent with this approach.[3]

Particularly in France,[4] but to varying degrees in other countries as well, mergers are encouraged or tolerated as a way of setting the units of the national economy on a level equal to that of competitor nations. The active concern of policy makers in Europe is not the prevalence of

1. "Recent Supreme Court decisions go so far in prohibiting specific mergers that any potential merger of two substantial, healthy companies is logically subject to challenge under the new precedents." Max Ways, "Antitrust in an Era of Radical Change," *Fortune*, vol. 73, no. 3 (March 1966), p. 222.

2. "Europe's Trustbusters," *The Economist*, August 31, 1974, p. 52.

3. The major exception to the generally favorable or neutral policy abroad with respect to mergers is West Germany's 1973 amendment to its Law against Restraints of Competition. The amendment empowered the Federal Cartel Authority to prohibit mergers that "may create or further strengthen a position of market dominance." In its administration, the amendment appears to have had little effect. Jürgen F. Baur, "The Control of Mergers between Large, Financially Strong Firms in West Germany," *Zeitschrift für die gesamte Staatswissenschaft*, vol. 136, no. 3 (September 1980), p. 444. In contrast, American policy has been to prevent further concentration. In the words of the Supreme Court, our policy is to arrest mergers "at a time when the trend to a lessening of competition in a line of commerce was still in its incipiency." U.S. v. Brown Shoe, 370 U.S. 317 (1962).

4. Frederic Jenny and André-Paul Weber, "French Antitrust Legislation: An Exercise in Futility," in Alexis P. Jacquemin and Henry W. de Jong, eds., *Welfare Aspects of Industrial Markets* (Leiden: Martinus Nijhoff, 1977).

1

industrial concentration but rather the handicap of inefficient, under-sized industrial units. Frederic M. Scherer, noting attitudes in other countries, remarks that

> those who read extensively in both the American and European industrial organization literature cannot avoid being struck by the contrast in emphasis. American economists seldom get very excited about scale economies, while for the typical European industry analyst, the day begins and ends with an impassioned tract on the advantages of size.[5]

The Growth in Relative Size of Foreign Competitors

The concentration policies of America's competitor nations allow, and often promote, the growth of their firms to the size of the larger U.S. firms (see table 1). European and Japanese corporations are now approaching, and in some cases have surpassed, their American rivals in size (and in their capacity for innovation). In 1967 twelve of the world's leading fifty industrial firms were foreign; today twenty-seven are. Foreign firms in the top fifty more than doubled in number in the past decade. The increased representation of European and Japanese chemical, electrical, and automobile firms is particularly noteworthy.

In diverse industries, U.S. firms are losing ground to their foreign competitors. In banking, for example, six of the eight leading banks of the world were, in 1960, U.S. firms. Now only two of the eight leading banks are domiciled in the United States. In metal manufacturing, seven of eight leading firms were based in the United States in 1960. Now only three are. While some of this change is due to economic factors that are independent of national concentration policies, it should be noted that new firms created through mergers have taken some top positions (Nippon Steel, Peugeot-Citröen, and Elf Aquitaine). Similar mergers in the United States are prohibited.

The somewhat more favorable attitude abroad toward mergers and increases in firm size augments the factors that work to the benefit of many overseas firms. This does not, to be sure, provide a justification for adopting wholesale the industrial policies of competitor nations. Many influences besides government policies govern the changes in the size and commercial success of firms. It should also be cautioned that the policies that promote size abroad at times do so at the expense of efficiency by converting what ought to be economic decisions into political ones. Subsidization and nationalization of firms

5. Frederic M. Scherer, *Industrial Market Structure and Economic Performance* (Chicago: Rand McNally, 1970), p. 93.

TABLE 1

RELATIVE SIZE OF 100 LEADING FOREIGN INDUSTRIAL FIRMS AND
100 LEADING U.S. INDUSTRIAL FIRMS,
BY GROUP, 1965, 1977, AND 1980

Firm Group (by rank)	Ratio of Foreign Firms' Sales to U.S. Firms' Sales		Ratio of Foreign Firms' Total Assets to U.S. Firms' Total Assets	
	$ billion	Percentage	$ billion	Percentage
	1965			
1–10	29/75	38	34/65	51
11–25	18/36	49	14/33	43
26–50	22/37	59	26/29	90
51–100	30/44	68	33/41	82
1–100	99/192	52	107/169	63
	1977			
1–10	164/298	55	139/193	72
11–25	131/130	101	123/119	104
26–50	131/129	102	118/84	140
51–100	163/159	103	194/123	158
1–100	589/716	82	574/519	111
	1980			
1–10	300/452	66	248/281	88
11–25	232/215	108	196/169	116
26–50	224/206	109	211/149	142
51–100	261/241	108	239/166	144
1–100	1,017/1,114	91	895/765	117

SOURCE: *Fortune*, May–August 1966, 1978, and 1981.

have had unhappy consequences. The current difficulties of the British Steel Corporation are illustrative. It can be argued, however, that a good deal of the more productive aspects of European policy are aimed at remedying the economic fragmentation of Europe. This appears to be sound policy, just as it would be sound policy for the United States to remove internal restrictions (such as those on branch banking at the state level and across state lines) and to pursue an essentially neutral policy toward both aggregate and market concentration.

The Conclusions of This Study

The following pages suggest the case for neutrality in U.S. merger policy. The changing size and character of successive merger movements in the United States are described. Their impact on industrial and aggregate concentration is analyzed. Horizontal mergers, which were common before the enactment in 1950 of the Celler-Kefauver amendment to the Clayton Act, show no detectable effect on industrial concentration. Conglomerate mergers, the predominant type of acquisition since the 1950s, show no influence on aggregate concentration and no negative influence on the number of businesses in operation. If anything, they have had a positive influence. They may also have brought the economies of size to firms small in their industries. This should appeal to those who prefer that the output of any one industry be dispersed among many firms. With the economies of size made available through conglomeration, many industries in which conglomerates operate are less concentrated than they would have been if conglomerates had not been allowed to enter through merger.

I also analyze the influence of conglomerate mergers on efficiency and the influence of corporate size on the ability to exercise economic and political power. Although some argue that conglomerate marriages among firms have no redeeming social value and simply reflect the megalomania of corporate empire builders, the data contradict this view of merger motivation.[6] The few analyses of political power that have been performed fail to demonstrate any ability by large corporations to exert disproportionate political influence.

The conclusion that follows from the analysis is that the merger guidelines issued by the Department of Justice in 1968 are misguided.[7] They are in need of the revision presently being undertaken, both to accord with economic realities and to take into account what the courts increasingly allow in light of those realities.[8] But there is a real question whether any guidelines should be written in terms of forbidding mergers that happen to be between firms that possess more than some threshold market share. It would be preferable to set the limits in terms of which mergers will be allowed without question rather than which mergers will be forbidden—a suggestion made in 1969 by the Presidential Task Force on Productivity and Competition.[9]

6. David J. Teece, "Horizontal Integration in Energy: Organizational and Technological Considerations," in W. Sid Moore, ed., *Horizontal Divestiture* (Washington, D.C.: American Enterprise Institute, 1977). For assertions that motives other than efficiency enhancement are the primary reasons for mergers, see Peter Behr, "Playing It Safe, and Losing Out," *Washington Post*, January 17, 1982.

7. See table 16 for a summary of the Department of Justice guidelines for mergers. See also, "Report of the Task Force on Productivity and Competition," *Congressional Record*, vol. 115 (June 16, 1969), p. 6475, for critical analysis of the guidelines.

8. Betty Bock, *Antitrust and the Supreme Court—An Economic Exploration* (New York: Conference Board, 1980), pp. 5–6.

9. Harold Demsetz, "Why Regulate Utilities?" *Journal of Law and Economics*, vol. 11 (April 1968); John S. McGee, *In Defense of Industrial Concentration* (New York: Praeger, 1971); Eugene F. Fama and Arthur B. Laffer, "The Number of Firms and Competition," *American Economic Review*, vol. 62 (September 1972); G. C. Archibald, " 'Large' and 'Small' Numbers in the Theory of the Firm," *Manchester School of Economics and Social*

The major fault inherent in the use of guidelines to prohibit certain classes of mergers is that they assume that a market concentration measure is an index of the probability of tacit collusion, but its usefulness for that purpose is much doubted.[10] They are based on disproved assumptions concerning the causes and effects of industrial concentration. They do not fit a world in which markets are international, with competition as common across as within national boundaries.

Studies, vol. 27 (January 1959); Edward Chadwick, "Results of Different Principles of Legislation and Administration in Europe; of Competition for the Field, as Compared with the Competition within the Field of Service," *Journal of the Royal Statistical Society*, vol. 22 (September 1859); Joan Bodoff, "Monopoly and Price Revisited," in Yale Brozen, ed., *The Competitive Economy: Selected Readings* (Morristown, N.J.: General Learning Press, 1975); Richard A. Posner, "Oligopoly and the Antitrust Laws: A Suggested Approach," *Stanford Law Review*, vol. 21 (June 1969); Peter Asch and Joseph J. Seneca, "Is Collusion Profitable?" *Review of Economics and Statistics*, vol. 58 (February 1976); and John R. Carter, "Antitrust, Competition, and the Demise of the Concentration Doctrine," *University of Toledo Law Review*, vol. 12 (Winter 1981).

10. Yale Brozen, *Industrial Concentration and Public Policy* (New York: Free Press, Macmillan, forthcoming).

2

A Perspective on Mergers

Corporate merger activity made its splashiest headlines of at least a decade during the bidding wars for Conoco, the nation's ninth largest oil company, and for Marathon, the nation's seventeenth largest oil company. Although the amount paid by du Pont for the Conoco shares it acquired in 1981 set a new record, $7.3 billion, that record was as much the result of inflation as it was of the size of the acquisition. The du Pont bid appears less awesome when we measure it and previous mergers in constant dollars. The all-time record measured in constant dollars was set as long ago as 1901, when U.S. Steel exchanged $17 billion in securities, in today's dollars, for the companies it consolidated.

Merger Waves and Their Size

Historians have recorded three distinct merger waves. A late-nineteenth-century wave crested in the five years 1898–1902, when recorded merger values in manufacturing and mining amounted to $6.3 billion.[1] Carl Eis found that assets of companies acquired in the five years 1926–1930, the crest of the 1920s merger wave, amounted to $7.3 billion.[2] The Federal Trade Commission (FTC) reported that the total assets of large manufacturing and mining acquisitions (firms with assets of $10 million or more) amounted to $46 billion in the 1966–1970 period, the crest of the 1960s merger wave.[3] And we seem now to be in the midst of a fourth merger wave. Acting Chairman David Clanton of the FTC testified before a House subcommittee that the amount paid in all merger transactions in the first half of 1981, before the occurrence of

1. Ralph L. Nelson, *Merger Movements in American Industry, 1895–1956* (Princeton: Princeton University Press, 1959), p. 37.

2. Carl Eis, "The 1919–1930 Merger Movement in American Industry," *Journal of Law and Economics*, vol. 12, no. 2 (October 1969), p. 271.

3. Federal Trade Commission, Bureau of Economics, *Statistical Report on Mergers and Acquisitions* (November 1976), p. 95.

the contest among du Pont, Mobil, and Seagram for Conoco, was $35.7 billion. He compared this with the total amount paid in the full year 1975 of $11.8 billion.[4]

Because of the declining value of the dollar and the growth in the size of the economy, these increasingly large nominal values in the successive merger waves exaggerate the relative size of the later transactions. Although the U.S. Steel consolidation is measured at $17 billion in today's dollars, the securities it issued at the time amounted to only $1.36 billion. The total book value of $6.3 billion for the manufacturing and mining assets acquired in 1898–1902 mergers would be $80 billion in today's dollars (and the value of the securities exchanged for these assets would be even greater).

To gain an appropriate perspective, we should measure the size of each episode in relation to the size of the manufacturing and mining sector. The turn-of-the-century consolidations in the five years 1898–1902 added up to 53 percent of the book value of all manufacturing and mining corporations. The recorded acquisitions of the late 1920s measured 9 percent of all corporate manufacturing and mining assets. The medium and large acquisitions of the latter 1960s came to 8 percent of such assets.

Simply looking at either the total nominal value of manufacturing and mining assets changing hands or the percentage of all such assets, however, tends to overstate the actual magnitude of control over assets attained by acquiring firms. There is double counting involved in simply adding together the value of every acquisition in a five-year interval. An acquisition by one firm is often either a part of a later acquisition by another or a later divestiture by that firm. U.S. Steel, for example, was a 1901 consolidation of ten consolidations. Assets merged in nine earlier consolidations in the steel industry in the years 1898–1900 were counted again in the 1901 U.S. Steel combination for the 1898–1902 total.

Frequently parts of an acquisition are divested by the acquiring firm. Since the acquisition of a divestiture is incorporated into the total count of acquired assets, this too results in double counting. In 1967 divestitures accounted for 11 percent of all mergers and acquisitions by

4. FTC *News Summary*, August 28, 1981. The book value of the assets acquired in 1975 was approximately $6 billion. The amount paid for acquired companies increased to $20 billion in 1976, $22 billion in 1977, $34 billion in 1978 (for 2,106 acquisitions), $43 billion in 1979, and $44 billion in 1980 (for 1,889 acquisitions). In the first nine months of 1981, merger activity totaled $61 billion. These figures were compiled by W. T. Grimm and Co. For earlier data on the number of acquisitions, see Gregg A. Jarrell and Michael Bradley, "The Economic Effects of Federal and State Regulations of Cash Tender Offers," *Journal of Law and Economics*, vol. 23, no. 2 (October 1980), table 5, p. 400.

number. They mounted to 39 percent in 1973 and to 54 percent in 1975. Although they then began a decline to 45 percent in 1977, they still amounted to 35 percent in 1979.[5]

The result of adding all assets in all mergers in any period covering five years, as we did in each of the instances described above, is to count some assets two or three times if the same assets are involved in two or three successive mergers. In the primary metal industry, for example, Ralph Nelson found that the sum of assets in all mergers from 1895 to 1907 in that industry amounted to 210 percent of the industry's assets,[6] an obvious case of double and triple counting.[7]

The Changing Character of Mergers

Our successive merger waves have, in addition to becoming progressively smaller in relative terms, also changed character. The consolidations occurring as we entered the twentieth century were largely horizontal combinations. That is, firms merged that produced the same products and sold in the same markets. They were competitors. Some were conglomerate combinations although they produced and sold the same products. Because they sold their products in different markets, we refer to these combinations as chain or market-extension mergers—one variety of the conglomerate merger.

The mergers of the 1920s were more often conglomerate or vertical mergers than the turn-of-the-century consolidations, and they were more often acquisitions than consolidations. Conglomerate mergers include several subcategories—market-extension, product-extension, and pure conglomerate. When Borden Company, operating a dairy in

5. W. T. Grimm data cited in J. W. Bradley and D. H. Korn, *Acquisition and Corporate Development* (Lexington, Mass.: D. C. Heath and Company, 1981), p. 8.

6. Nelson, *Merger Movements*, table D-1, p. 171.

7. A comparison of the proportion of all manufacturing assets in the hands of consolidations at a given point in time with the sum of all mergers in a preceding period as a proportion of all assets yields another indication of the double counting involved in adding together each and every merger in a given time span. Walter Adams reports that the 300 industrial combinations in existence in 1904 "controlled fully 40 percent of the nation's manufacturing capital." [Walter Adams, "Comment on Markham's Survey of the Evidence and Findings on Mergers," in National Bureau of Economic Research, *Business Concentration and Price Policy* (Princeton, N.J.: Princeton University Press, 1955), p. 183.] Although some of these, such as Standard Oil, American Tobacco, U.S. Rubber, Pittsburgh Plate Glass, and American Sugar Refining, were created before 1898, Nelson reports that the book value of mergers for 1898–1902 came to 53 percent of all corporate manufacturing and mining assets. Some of the consolidations late in the five-year period were consolidations of earlier consolidations occurring in the same time span, thus counting the earlier consolidations twice. See Nelson, *Merger Movements*, table C-6, p. 163, for examples.

8

New York City, acquired a dairy in another city to which it shipped none of its fluid milk products, the merger was classified as a market-extension acquisition. When Procter and Gamble acquired Clorox, which sold liquid bleach to the same grocery stores to which Procter and Gamble sold soap, this was categorized as a product-extension merger. And when United Aircraft bought the Otis Elevator Company, the transaction was classified as a pure conglomerate merger.

In addition to being predominantly horizontal, late-nineteenth-century mergers were also, to a large extent, simultaneous consolidations of several companies. That is, three or more firms were combined to form a new corporate entity. "Seventy-five percent of 1895–1904 firm disappearances took place by the consolidation of five or more firms."[8] In the 1920s, consolidations accounted for only 30 percent of merger value and 36 percent of firm disappearances.[9] By the 1960s, consolidations became rare events.

In the 1960s merger wave, conglomerate acquisitions dominated in contrast to the dominance of horizontal acquisitions in the 1920s (see table 2) and their even greater importance around 1900, when almost industrywide consolidations were abundant. The change after 1950 was largely a consequence of the 1950 Celler-Kefauver antimerger amendment to the Clayton Act.[10]

Mergers and Industrial Concentration

The Celler-Kefauver amendment was passed in 1950 at the urging of the Federal Trade Commission. The commission had concluded, in a 1948 report on mergers: "If nothing is done to check the growth in concentration...the giant corporations will ultimately take over the country....[Without] the proposed amendment to the Clayton Act,...the rise in economic concentration cannot be checked."[11]

The Federal Trade Commission staff was mistaken in its view that a "rise in economic concentration" was taking place. Morris A. Adelman, reviewing material in the FTC staff report, tells us that the number of mergers in the years preceding the report was lower than in earlier years. "The Commission, however, for reasons not explained in its report, interpreted the low rate of mergers as evidence that the

8. Nelson, *Merger Movements*, p. 29.

9. Eis, "The 1919–1930 Merger Movement," p. 279.

10. Staff of the Bureau of Economics, Federal Trade Commission, "The Celler-Kefauver Act: Sixteen Years of Enforcement," *Economic Papers 1966–1969* (1970, pp. 32–82.

11. Federal Trade Commission, *The Merger Movement: A Summary Report* (1948), p. 28.

TABLE 2
DISTRIBUTION OF MEDIUM AND LARGE MERGER DISAPPEARANCES, BY TYPE OF ACQUISITION, 1926–1979
(percent)

Type of Merger	1926–30	1940–47[a]	1948–53	1954–64	1965–79
Horizontal[b]	64	62	31	18	14
Vertical	5	17	10	15	8
Conglomerate	31	21	59	67	78
Market extension	(12)	[c]	(7)	(7)	(3)
Product extension and other	(19)	(21)	(52)	(60)	(75)
Total	100	100	100	100	100
Number of disappearances classified	486[d]	2,062	58	662	1,426[e]

a. Includes small mergers as well as medium and large acquisitions.

b. Quite a number of mergers classified by the FTC as horizontal involved very small product overlaps. In many of these mergers, the largest proportion of the product of the acquired firm was vertically related or was a product extension.

c. For this period, the FTC included market-extension mergers in the horizontal group.

d. Eis found the total number of manufacturing and mining companies acquired in this period (reported in the press) to be 1,946. Only the larger acquisitions were categorized. W. L. Thorp, using Standard Corporation records, reports 4,838 manufacturing and mining firms acquired in this period.

e. Not included in the tabulation of acquired firms with assets of $10 million or more are companies for which data were not publicly available. There were 382 such companies for the period 1965–1979 and 137 for the period 1948–1964. The rise in annual number of acquisitions from ten in 1948–1953 to sixty in 1954–1964 to ninety-five in 1965–1979 overstates the actual rise in medium and large acquisitions since the $10 million cutoff was stated in current, not constant, dollars.

SOURCES: Eis, "The 1919–1930 Merger Movement," p. 294, table 16; and Federal Trade Commission, Bureau of Economics, *Statistical Report on Mergers and Acquisitions*, p. 115, table 18.

mergers were actually 'increasing concentration' and 'strengthening the position of big business.'"[12] Adelman rebuts the commission's conclusions, reporting that, "the painstaking work of Lintner and Butters has shown that the 1940–47 merger movement had little or no effect on concentration."[13]

12. Morris·A. Adelman, "The Measurement of Industrial Concentration," *Review of Economics and Statistics*, vol. 33 (November 1951), p. 294.

13. Ibid.

Not only Adelman has criticized this piece of FTC research; Justice Potter Stewart, dissenting in *U.S.* v. *Von's Grocery Co.*, said:

> Much of the fuel for the congressional debates on concentration in the American economy [before the passage of the Celler-Kefauver amendment to the Clayton Act] was derived from a contemporary study by the Federal Trade Commission on corporate acquisitions between 1940 and 1947. See Report of the Federal Trade Commission on the Merger Movement: A Summary Report (1948). A critical study of the FTC report, published while the 1950 amendment was pending in Congress, concluded that the effect of the recent merger movement on concentration had been slight. Lintner & Butters, Effect of Mergers on Industrial Concentration, 1940–1947, 32 *Rev. of Econ. & Statistics* 30 (1950). Two economists for the Federal Trade Commission later acquiesced in that conclusion. Blair & Houghton, The Lintner-Butters Analysis of the Effect of Mergers on Industrial Concentration 1940–1947, 33 *Rev. of Econ. & Statistics* 63, 67, no. 12 (1951).[14]

In the same article in which he impeached the FTC summary report *The Merger Movement*, Adelman also examined the Federal Trade Commission *Report on the Concentration of Productive Facilities, 1947*.[15] He found that the conceptual basis of the measure of concentration used was inadequate and produced misleading results.

> The report used. . . "net capital assets" as the best measure of size and concentration and applied it to 26 industries, despite the fact that this measure accounts for only one-third of all assets. Some explanation is obviously necessary for this omission of two-thirds of the information. . . .
>
> The exclusion of inventories—part of the "ideal" figure—from the measure of concentration is the strangest part of the whole procedure. It is explained as follows:
>
> "According to reports of the Senate Small Business Committee, numerous small firms experienced great difficulty during that year [1947] in obtaining adequate inventories of raw materials. If inventories were thus relatively shorter in small than in large firms—as there is every reason to believe was the case—the inclusion of inventories in the measure

14. U.S. v. Von's Grocery Co., 384 U.S. 284, n. 6 (1966). See also Derek C. Bok, "Section 7 of the Clayton Act and the Merging of Law and Economics," *Harvard Law Review*, vol. 74 (1960).

15. Federal Trade Commission, *Report on the Concentration of Productive Facilities, 1947* (1949), p. 7.

would have the effect of overstating the degree of economic concentration."

Setting aside the question of the reliability of the evidence, our concern is with the logic of the procedure. A glance at Table I will show that the over-$100 million group held 35.6 per cent of inventories. According to the report, this was an abnormally high percentage. In a more representative year, that is, it would be lower. Suppose we were to disregard this qualification for the moment, and add inventories to net capital assets to obtain net tangible assets—the "ideal" figure—as a measure of concentration. Then the percentage held by the largest corporations would be not 46.1 per cent but 41.1. But in a normal year, according to the report, the largest corporations would have held a smaller proportion of inventories than 35.6 per cent and therefore a smaller proportion of total tangible assets than 41.1 per cent. The FTC explanation can therefore be paraphrased as follows: to have used the estimate of 41.1 per cent would have resulted in an overestimate of the degree of concentration; therefore, we are using an estimate of 46.1![16]

That the FTC reports in 1948 and 1949 were mistaken in their conclusions is further demonstrated by Bureau of the Census data on concentration that have become available. Although the 1940–1947 period was characterized by the FTC in its 1948 report as a third merger wave rivaling the turn-of-the-century and the 1920s waves, with the acquisition of more than 2,000 firms, the average concentration ratio was unaffected. It was 40.2 percent in 1935 (see table 3) in the 272 industry groups for which the Bureau of the Census disclosed concentration data. The bureau used 281 groups for all manufacturing. On the basis of a minimum estimate of concentration in the remaining nine industries, the average concentration ratio was 41.8. It failed to rise by 1947 despite a finer subdivision of manufacturing into 463 industries by the bureau in its 1947 measurement. Although this finer subdivision would be expected to raise the average concentration ratio, average concentration fell to 39.7 percent in 1947.

Examining the 126 industries with unchanged definitions from 1935 to 1947, we find that the majority of highly concentrated industries became less concentrated despite the permissive merger policy of the period. The majority of those that were unconcentrated became more concentrated. This convergence toward the average concentration ratio apparently was the consequence of a centripetal tendency. The same tendency also characterized the later period, 1947 to

16. Adelman, "Measurement of Concentration," p. 274.

TABLE 3

Distribution of Manufacturers' Shipments, by Four-Firm Concentration, 1935, 1972, and 1977

Four-Firm Concentration	Percentage Share of Shipments[a]		
	1935[b]	1972	1977
0–9.9	16.6 (20)	5.4 (17)	6.0 (20)
10–19.9	13.5 (40)	16.4 (70)	17.0 (72)
20–29.9	17.0 (44)	20.0 (97)	16.8 (96)
30–39.9	14.5 (50)	14.8 (72)	18.4 (68)
40–49.9	10.6 (31)	10.9 (61)	11.0 (64)
50–59.9	6.9 (25)	10.7 (57)	11.0 (58)
60–69.9	7.6 (26)	9.1 (28)	7.4 (30)
70–79.9	2.8 (17)	4.1 (26)	4.2 (18)
80–89.9	9.2 (18)[c]	1.4 (11)	2.5 (19)[d]
90–100	0.2 (4)[e]	7.2 (11)[f]	5.8 (4)[g]
0–59.9	79.1 (210)	78.2 (374)	80.2 (378)
60–100	20.9 (71)[h]	21.8 (76)	19.8 (71)
Weighted average concentration	37.0 (272)	40.2 (450)	39.1 (446)
Simple average concentration	40.2 (272)[i]	39.1 (450)	38.4 (446)

a. Number of industries in each group is in parentheses. The census has 451 manufacturing industries in its 1972 Standard Industrial Classification code, but it combined industries 3572 and 3579 in calculating concentration ratios for 1972 and 1977.
b. Does not add to 100 because of the omission of six industries whose concentration was not disclosed. The Bureau of the Census combined eighty-two textiles-and-their-products industries into twenty-two for its concentration report.
c. Industry 1003 included here but not in the calculation of average concentration in all manufacturing.
d. Industries 2111 and 3661 are included here (although the Bureau of the Census did not disclose four-firm concentration data for these industries) but not in the calculation of average concentration in all manufacturing for 1977.
e. Industries 624 and 1314 included in this group but not in the calculation of average concentration for all manufacturing for lack of precise four-firm concentration figures. The six industries omitted for lack of data probably belong in this group. If they were included, the share of shipments would be 1.3.
f. For SIC 3661, telephone and telegraph apparatus, the 1970 figure of 94 was used since the Census Bureau did not disclose the figure for 1972.
g. Industry 2823 included here (although the four-firm concentration figure was not disclosed) but not in average concentration in all manufacturing.
h. Includes six industries for which concentration data were not disclosed.
i. If we include nine industries for which concentration data were not disclosed at their minimum concentration ratios, the simple average becomes 41.8 instead of 40.2.

Sources: U.S. Department of Commerce, Bureau of the Census, *Census of Manufactures, 1972, Concentration Ratios in Manufacturing*, MC76 (SR)-2 (Washington, D.C., October 1975), table 5; Bureau of the Census, *Concentration Ratios in Manufacturing* (May 1981), table 7; and U.S. National Resources Committee, *The Structure of the American Economy* (June 1939), table 1, p. 265.

1977, when important horizontal mergers were no longer permitted (see table 4).[17] Among those industries in which four firms shipped 75 percent or more of their industry's product in 1935, concentration decreased in 53 percent by 1947. It increased in only 24 percent. In the industries where concentration was 24 percent or less, concentration decreased in 20 percent and increased in 52 percent. Walter Adams observes, of this period, that "here indeed is an eloquent testimonial to the dynamism and competitiveness of the American economy. Here indeed is a graphic manifestation of the competitive forces in the economy—holding their own despite a public policy which left the highway to monopoly [horizontal mergers] unblocked and un-guarded."[18]

To Adams's observation, we can add that mergers since the turn of the century, as well as those of the 1935–1947 period, apparently did not increase average industrial concentration, despite their pre-dominantly horizontal character up to the 1950s. Warren Nutter esti-mated that 33 percent of manufacturing value added between 1895 and 1904 came from industries whose four-firm concentration ratio ex-ceeded 50 percent.[19] By 1954 the share of value added in manufacturing by industries more than 50 percent concentrated *dropped* to 30 percent.[20] Whether we look at periods in which merger policy was very permissive or at those in which it was very restrictive, general trends in concentration are largely the same, apparently unaffected by the nature of policy.

The Legacy of the Turn-of-the-Century Merger Movement

Economists and statisticians have, in times past, argued that the consolidations late in the nineteenth century (which created firms with market shares greater than 50 percent in seventy-eight industries, in twenty-six of which corporations had been formed with market shares of more than 80 percent) left a permanent stamp on the structure of American industry. But the fact is that the horizontal consolidations in

17. What we have called here a "centripetal tendency" is the equivalent of what statisticians call the "regression phenomenon." It is a result of the probability that highly concentrated industries more frequently have a concentration ratio above the equi-librium (efficient) level while low concentration industries more frequently are below the equilibrium level.

18. Adams, "Comment," p. 190.

19. Warren Nutter, *The Extent of Enterprise Monopoly in the United States: 1899–1939* (Chicago: University of Chicago Press, 1951), p. 147.

20. Frederic M. Scherer, *Industrial Market Structure and Economic Performance*, 2d ed. (Chicago: Rand McNally, 1980), p. 68.

TABLE 4

INDUSTRIES WITH RISING, STABLE, OR DECLINING CONCENTRATION,
BY CONCENTRATION LEVEL, 1947–1977

Concentration Range in 1947	Number of Industries in 1947[a]	Percentage Distribution		
		More than two percentage points increase in concentration, 1947–1977	Stable concentration, 1947–1977	More than two percentage points decrease in concentration, 1947–1977
0–24	59	61	24	15
25–49	52	50	15	35
50–74	32	28	6	66
75–100	19	21	11	68
Total	162			

a. The industries selected are all those for which concentration data are available whose definitions were essentially unchanged from 1947 to 1977 or in which changes did not produce material movements in concentration ratios contrary to those reported.
SOURCE: Bureau of the Census, *Concentration Ratios in Manufacturing* (1981).

15

the two decades through 1902 produced a structural legacy little different from what it would have been without the large consolidations.

In the industries where concentration produced efficiencies and the consolidations were efficiently managed, they remained pre-eminent, although their market shares declined as their industries grew (see table 5). In those industries where concentration did not produce efficiencies or the consolidations were not well managed, the combinations failed or had to be reorganized (see table 6). None succeeded in maintaining monopoly prices although some tried (notably American Sugar Refining, which owned 98 percent of the sugar-refining capacity east of the Rockies, and American Can, with 90 percent of the can-making capacity).[21]

That many industries and their customers benefited from the horizontal mergers is demonstrated by the price movement in industries with important consolidations in relation to those with minor consolidations and those with no consolidations. The National Industrial Conference Board found that in twenty-six industries in which important consolidations took place and for which price data were available, prices fell by 13 percent from 1900 to 1913 and then rose by 49 percent from 1913 to 1925. In twenty industries in which no consolidations occurred, prices rose by 10 percent from 1900 to 1913 and then rose another 96 percent from 1913 to 1925 (see figure 1).

There is a wide variation in the degree of concentration among U.S. manufacturing industries (see table 3). Differing economic characteristics in each of the many industries cause this wide variation. Today's industrial structure is a result of this variation in characteristics. Joe Bain found (as did Frederic L. Pryor in a later study) that industries that are concentrated in the United States are also concentrated in other countries. Those with low concentration are also the same abroad as in the United States.[22] This suggests that *fundamental technological and economic forces determine industry structure* and that it is little different today from what it would have been without the turn-of-the-century consolidations.

21. Richard Zerbe, "The American Sugar Refinery Company, 1887–1914: The Story of a Monopoly," *Journal of Law and Economics*, vol. 12, no. 2 (October 1969), pp. 339–75.

22. Joe S. Bain, *International Differences in Industrial Structure* (New Haven, Conn.: Yale University Press, 1966); Frederic L. Pryor, "An International Comparison of Concentration Ratios," *Review of Economics and Statistics*, vol. 54 (May 1972). Pryor concludes that "the data show that the average four-digit concentration ratios among *large* industrial nations are roughly the same. . . . The data show that the rank order of concentration ratios are roughly the same in all nations" (pp. 138–39). See also Peter Pashigian, "Market Concentration in the United States and Great Britain," *Journal of Law and Economics*, vol. 11 (October 1968).

TABLE 5

Market Shares of Selected
Turn-of-the-Century Combinations

Company	Early Share		Later Share	
	Percentage	Year	Percentage	Year
Standard Oil	88	1899	67	1909
American Sugar Refining	95	1892	75	1894
			49	1907
			28	1917
American Strawboard	85–90	1889	33	1919
National Starch Manufacturing	70	1890	45	1899
Glucose Sugar Refining	85	1897	45	1901
International Paper	66	1898	30	1911
			14	1928
American Tin Plate	95	1899	54	1912
American Writing Paper	75	1899	5	1952
American Tobacco[a]	93	1899	76	1903
American Can	90	1901	60	1903
U.S. Steel[b]	66	1901	46	1920
			33	1934
International Harvester[c]	85	1902	44	1922
			23	1948
American Smelting and Refining	85–95	1902	31	1937
Corn Products Refining	90	1906	59	1914

a. Share of cigarette sales.
b. Share based on steel ingot castings. A weighted average of ten products gives U.S. Steel 57 percent of the market in 1901, declining to 47 percent in 1913. Arthur S. Dewing, *Corporate Promotions and Reorganizations* (Cambridge: Harvard University Press, 1914), p. 527. U.S. Steel's share dwindled despite additional large acquisitions in 1904 and 1905.
c. Under a 1918 antitrust consent decree, Harvester disposed of its Champion and Osborne lines of harvesting machinery in 1919. These accounted for less than 10 percent of its output of four major implements and a smaller share of all farm machinery.
Source: Simon Whitney, *Antitrust Policies* (New York: Twentieth Century Fund, 1958).

In the absence of constraints on competition, such as those imposed by the private express statutes or monopoly utility franchises, concentrated industries are concentrated because that is the efficient way to organize them. Unconcentrated industries are unconcentrated because that is the efficient way to organize them. As Harold Demsetz has pointed out:

My own studies . . . indicate that the more *concentrated* the

TABLE 6

Consolidations with Large Market Shares Failing within a Few Years after Their Formation, 1890–1905

American Barrel & Package
American Bicycle
American Cement
American Cotton Company
American Electric Heating
American Felt
American Fisheries
American Fork & Hoe
American Fruit Products
American Grass Twine
American Laundry Machinery
American Malting
American Saddlery & Harness
American Wood Working
   Machinery
American Wringer
Asphalt Company of America
Atlantic Rubber Shoe Co. of
   America
Booth, A. & Co.
Consolidated Railway Lighting &
   Equipment
Consolidated Railway Lighting &
   Refrigeration
Consolidated Rubber Tire
Continental Cotton Oil
Corn Products Co.
Development Co. of America
Distillers & Cattle Feeders
Distilling Co. of America
Electric Vehicle Co.
General Roofing
Glucose Sugar Refining Co.
Great Western Cereal
International Car Wheel
Mt. Vernon–Woodberry Cotton
   Duck

National Asphalt
National Cordage
National Glass
National Novelty
National Shear
National Starch
National Wallpaper
New England Yarn
Pope Manufacturing
Standard Rope & Twine
United Box Board & Paper
United Button Company
United Copper Company
United Zinc & Lead
U.S. Cotton Duck
U.S. Dyewood & Extract
U.S. Finishing
U.S. Leather
U.S. Reduction & Refining
U.S. Shipbuilding
U.S. Worsted

Rejuvenations
Allis Chalmers
American Colortype
American School Furniture
American Soda Fountain
Central Foundry
International Fire Engine
National Salt
U.S. Cast Iron Pipe
U.S. Flour Milling
U.S. Realty & Improvement

NOTE: These companies were classified as early failures on the basis that creditors suffered a loss within a decade after formation. The ten "rejuvenations" are classified separately on the basis of "a successful existence...subsequent to changes in capital set-up."

SOURCE: Shaw Livermore, "The Success of Industrial Mergers," *Quarterly Journal of Economics*, vol. 50 (November 1935), p. 90.

FIGURE 1

PRICE FLUCTUATIONS IN THREE GROUPS OF MANUFACTURING
INDUSTRIES, 1900–1925
(1900 = 100)

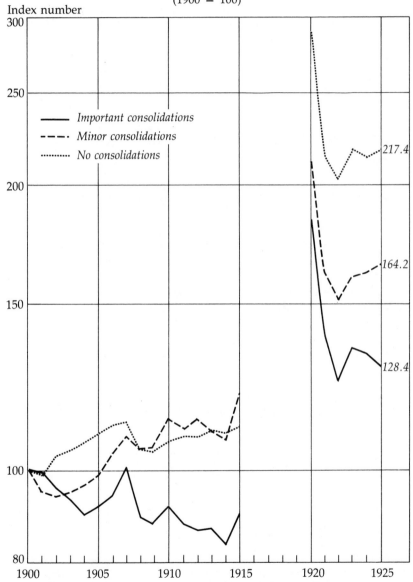

SOURCE: National Industrial Conference Board, *Mergers in Industry: A Study of Certain Economic Aspects of Industrial Consolidation* (New York: National Industrial Conference Board, 1929), p. 146.

industry, the lower are the costs of large firms relative to the costs of medium and small firms in those industries; this difference in costs is substantial. The cost advantage diminishes to insignificance for very *unconcentrated* industries. I believe that is why one set of industries is and remains concentrated and the other does not. This suggests that where concentration is found, it is largely a consequence of the competitive process, and that such industry structures are derived from those techniques yielding low-cost production. Competition would have altered concentrated structures if there were no associated efficiencies; in fact, many industries remain unconcentrated or have become unconcentrated because no special efficiencies or entrepreneurial successes have called forth and maintained concentrated structures.[23]

That concentrated industries and firms with large market shares are not entrenched in their positions is demonstrated by postwar experience as well by the experience of the late nineteenth and early twentieth centuries shown in tables 5 and 6. In the period from 1947 to 1977, there were forty-five episodes in which highly concentrated four-digit industries experienced decreases of ten points or more in the share of business done by the leading four firms in those industries (see table 7). These occurred in thirty-nine of seventy-two highly concentrated industries.[24] Examining the incomplete data for five-digit product classes for 1947–1972, we find more than 240 cases of decreases in four-firm concentration ratios of ten percentage points or more. These experiences substantiate Demsetz's conclusion that "competition . . . alter[s] concentrated structures if there [are] no associated efficiencies."[25]

23. Harold Demsetz, "The Trust upon Which Antitrust Stands," *Antitrust Law Journal*, vol. 46, issue 3 (Summer 1977), p. 821.

24. Competition also results in increases in the market shares of leading firms where they are more efficient and innovative than their competitors and pass some of the benefits of efficiency and innovation on to their customers. In the seventy-two industries analyzed that were more than 70 percent concentrated at some time between 1947 and 1977, there were eleven episdoes in which the share of domestic output produced by the four leading firms increased by ten percentage points or more. Frequently a different set of four firms constituted the leading four at a later time than those appearing among the leading four earlier. The Bureau of the Census reported changes in composition of the leading four firms for a large set of industries only for 1947 and 1958. This prevents us from knowing how slippery is the grasp of a leading firm on its position in its industry. Even in this short interval, however, at least one of the four leading firms dropped out of the group in 81 percent of the 204 industries for which the bureau reported data. This is strong evidence that leading firms are not entrenched in their positions and that achievement of a leading position by the merger route is no guarantee that competition is ended by the acquisition of competitors or that an industry's structure is permanently changed by mergers.

25. Demsetz, "The Trust upon Which Antitrust Stands," p. 821.

Competition is constantly at work altering industry structures, moving them toward their equilibriums, which are themselves being moved by changing circumstances. A changing structural equilibrium results from changes in tastes, resources, technology, or institutional factors (such as tariffs and government regulations). Industrial structure is neither arbitrary nor immutable. Rather it is the result of efforts by market participants to achieve their ends at least cost and, as changes in a variety of industries demonstrate, is influenced by changing conditions.

Conclusion

Apparently there need be little concern about horizontal mergers. Where they are inefficient and yield no benefit to their customers, their market share soon dwindles. Where they are efficient, they persist, and their customers benefit. To forbid horizontal mergers simply causes an industry to approach its efficient structure by a more costly route. It forecloses the opportunity for smaller firms to sell out on favorable terms. "The principal effect of a very strict rule against horizontal mergers is not to retard economic progress, it is to reduce the sale value of small firms."[26] Joe Bain adds that where the equilibrium structure of an industry is one of high concentration, a high

> degree of seller concentration would emerge more or less automatically as a result of competition even if sellers were initially many and small. If there are important economies of the large-scale firm, so that to approach optimal scale a firm must supply a significant fraction of the market, atomistic competition among many firms will lead all to expand. This expansion will drive price down until only large-scale firms can survive, eliminating all but a few firms, and will thus "automatically" produce an oligopolistic or concentrated market structure.[27]

Forbidding horizontal mergers, then, may simply force many firms into voluntary liquidation or bankruptcy (or into selling out to a conglomerate where the economies of size are not product specific). The capital invested in their facilities and organization is wasted while the growing firms commit capital to enlarging old plants or building

26. Richard A. Posner, *Antitrust Law: An Economic Perspective* (Chicago: University of Chicago Press, 1976), p. 105. For a contrary view, see Staff of the Bureau of Economics, Federal Trade Commission, "The Celler-Kefauver Act: Sixteen Years of Enforcement," *Economic Papers 1966–69* (1970), pp. 32–82.

27. Joe Bain, *Industrial Organization*, 2d ed. (New York: John Wiley and Sons, 1968), p. 183.

TABLE 7

Highly Concentrated Industries with Decreases of Ten Points or More in Industry or Product Group Concentration Ratios, 1947–1977

Four-Firm Share of Industry (I) or Product Group (P) Shipments

Industry	1947 I	1947 (P)	1954 I	1954 (P)	1958 I	1958 (P)	1963 I	1963 (P)	1967 I	1967 (P)	1972 I	1972 (P)	1977 I	1977 (P)
2045 Blended and prepared flour	77													
2046 Corn milling	72				70								51	
2052 Biscuits and crackers			64		59						63			
2085 Distilled liquor	75				58						47			
2111 Cigarettes	90					79								
2141 Tobacco stemming	88		73						63					
2271 Woven carpets											78		67	
2646 Molded pulp	86		72											
2811 Sulfuric acid	82			(D)								(55)		
2813 Industrial gases	84						72							
2824 Organic fibers							94		84		74			
2833 Medicinals and botanicals									74					
2841 Soap and detergents							72		70		59			
2861 Gum and wood chemicals									67		62			
2892 Explosives	79												59	
2898 Salt				(83)								(70)		
2999 Petroleum and coal products, n.e.c.									82				67	

SIC	Industry	I		P	
3021	Rubber footwear	81			
3031	Reclaimed rubber	84	73	65	
3229	Pressed glass, n.e.c.	93	78		61
3275	Gypsum products	90	80	93	71
3313	Electrometallurgical products	88			69
3331	Primary copper	73	87	79	77
3334	Primary aluminum	100			79
3352	Aluminum rolling	94	78	80	
3411	Metal cans	80	78		66
3463	Nonferrous forgings				71
3511	Turbines and generator sets	(70)	84		(56)
3568	Mechanical stokers	78	67	93	76
3574	Calculating machines		67		
3612	Transformers	78		83	73
3652	Phonograph records	79	68	58	59
3673	Electron tubes, transmitting	69	58	48	56
3723	Aircraft propellers		70		55
3932	Organs	(90)	81	(77)	
3933	Piano and organ parts	71			
3982	Cork products	84	(74)	(67)	(48)
		(D)		(48)	(46)

NOTE: The I column shows the four-firm concentration ratio in each industry at the time of the industry's peak concentration and at the subsequent time when it had dropped by at least ten percentage points. The (P) column shows similar data for product group concentration. n.e.c. = not elsewhere classified.

SOURCE: Bureau of the Census, *Concentration Ratios in Manufacturing* (May 1981), tables 7 and 9.

new ones—capital that could be applied to alternative uses instead of building redundant capacity.

The beer industry provides a classic example of the building of redundant capacity by growing firms because the merger route for acquiring additional capacity and for expanding into new markets was foreclosed. Despite the application of a strict antitrust enforcement policy against mergers, the concentration ratio in brewing rose from 11 percent in 1935 to 63 percent in 1977 (and the number of firms decreased from 756 in 1934 to 49 in 1976).[28]

The Federal Trade Commission's Bureau of Economics believes that antimerger policy may actually have promoted higher concentration in the industry. It says:

> The fact that mergers have accounted for such a small share of the increase in concentration is directly a result of very strict antitrust enforcement by the Justice Department. But this policy may have, in the end, promoted higher national concentration in two ways: (1) By foreclosing the merger route to the national brewers, it forced them to expand internally. As we have seen, their large new breweries are more efficient than the older smaller ones. . . . (2) The Department has blocked merger of smaller brewers. This may have had the effect of weakening the competitive position of the latter group of firms.[29]

The result of the large amount of new brewery capacity built by firms that were not allowed to buy existing breweries was that the industry found itself saddled with 40 percent excess capacity. Much of this was junked and the capital wasted.

This suggests that the new guidelines for horizontal mergers, which the Department of Justice intends to issue soon, should be much less strict than the 1968 limits it enunciated. The 1969 report of the Presidential Task Force on Productivity and Competition also argues that "the Department of Justice Merger Guidelines are extraordinarily stringent and in some respects indefensible."[30]

28. The same concentration trend in brewing has occurred in other countries as well as the United States, evidently responding to the same technological and economic forces as the U.S. industry. Concentration in the beer industry in Canada increased by thirty-eight percentage points between 1948 and 1972. In Great Britain the share of the five leading brewing firms increased from 23 to 64 percent from 1958 to 1968 (not necessarily the same five firms in 1968 as in 1958).

29. Federal Trade Commission, Bureau of Economics, *The Brewing Industry* (1979), pp. 64–65.

30. "Report of the Task Force on Productivity and Competition," *Congressional Record*, vol. 115 (June 16, 1969), p. 6475; reprinted in *Journal of Reprints for Antitrust Law and Economics*, vol. 1 (Winter 1969), pp. 829–81.

3
Conglomerate Mergers and Efficiency

In 1979, when Senator Howard Metzenbaum opened the hearings on S. 600, a bill designed to stop conglomerate mergers by corporations with assets or sales exceeding $350 million, he said:

> It's hard to make a convincing case that putting cigarettes, Hawaiian Punch and offshore oil and gas under one corporate umbrella will have any startling effects on the efficiency with which our economy operates. There is of course some argument about capital allocation, managerial skills, and so forth. But the consensus...among industrial or organizational economists, is that most large conglomerate mergers, are at best neutral, with respect to efficiency, and actually may have adverse effects in many instances.[1]

Neither Metzenbaum nor any witness at these hearings provided any evidence that conglomerate mergers do not improve efficiency. Dennis Mueller thought he provided such evidence by citing a survey of the research on the profitability of investing in the acquisition of companies. He testified that the survey showed that "no one who has undertaken a major empirical study of mergers has concluded that mergers are profitable, i.e., profitable in the sense of being 'more profitable' than alternative forms of investment." Mueller concluded "that mergers neither increase nor decrease economic efficiency on average."[2]

Financial Evidence That Mergers Improve Efficiency

That acquiring companies, on the average, earned only normal returns

1. U.S. Congress, Senate, Subcomitee on Antitrust, Monopoly, and Business Rights of the Committee on the Judiciary, *Hearings on Mergers and Economic Concentration*, 96th Congress, 1st session, 1979, serial no. 96-2, pt. 1, pp. 8–9 (hereafter *1979 S. 600 Hearings*).

2. *1979 S. 600 Hearings*, p. 304, statement of Dennis C. Mueller.

on their investments in acquisitions should not be surprising. The average return on *all* investments is equal to the normal return. Any class of investments on which above average returns can be earned does not long remain in that position unless knowledge of such investments is a secret. Once such investments have become known, investors bid their prices to the level where only normal returns are earned. If the market for acquisitions is competitive, then acquirers can be expected to earn only as much, on average, as they would earn in "alternative forms of investment."

Acquirers of firms listed on the New York Stock Exchange in the postwar years paid substantial premiums for their acquisitions. The premiums averaged 25 percent from 1955 through 1976 on the price prevailing before each merger or tender offer announcement.[3] Even these preoffer values were influenced by the expectation that a bid would be forthcoming. They would have been lower but for that expectation. For the firms acquired when there was no expectation that someone would offer to buy them (the merger offer came as a complete surprise), the premiums averaged more than 50 percent.[4] In recent years, premiums have trended upward, reaching 50 percent in 1979.

The fact that premiums were paid suggests that the acquirers expected to use the acquired assets more efficiently than they had previously been used. Premiums would be offered only if the buying firms expected to produce returns of greater value to their stockholders than the value to the acquired firms' stockholders of the expected returns under the old managements. Since the acquirers' stockholders enjoyed returns after the mergers roughly equal to those of all New York Stock Exchange firms (see figure 2), the expectations were accurate. A marked improvement in the value of the returns must have occurred after the acquisition; otherwise the premiums paid would have produced losses in the acquiring companies. They would have suffered below normal returns, with a consequent loss to their stockholders if the premiums had not been subsequently justified and their value sustained by improvements in efficiency.

Paul Asquith points out that findings in his study of postwar mergers show that

> mergers cause a change in real activity, and this change produces a real gain for the combined firm. That is, the firms

3. Paul Asquith, "A Two-Event Study of Merger Bids, Market Uncertainty, and Stockholder Returns" (Ph.D. dissertation, Graduate School of Business, University of Chicago, 1980), tables 6, 12, pp. 26, 35.

4. Ibid., table 27, p. 52. For all takeovers in the United Kingdom from 1957 to 1969, the average premium was 64.9 percent. See Douglas A. Kuehn, *Takeovers and the Theory of the Firm* (London: Macmillan, 1975).

FIGURE 2

Returns to Stockholders of Acquiring Firms in Relation to the Average New York Stock Exchange Firm

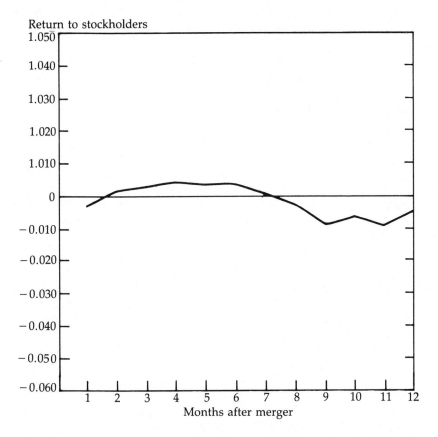

NOTE: Figure shows monthly cumulative average residual return to stockholders of acquiring firms after completion of merger (in percentage of investment in acquiring firm at date of merger).
SOURCE: Paul Asquith, "Mergers and the Market for Acquisitions," mimeographed (January 1979).

are worth more when they are combined than when they are alone. . . .

Furthermore, the results suggest that the resource which is being acquired in a merger is . . . [an] inefficient[ly] man-age[d] . . . target firm.[5]

5. Asquith, "Study of Merger Bids," pp. 2–3.

Other Evidence of Conglomerate Efficiency

That conglomerates are more efficient, or at least use their labor more productively, than single-industry enterprises was demonstrated by Victor Fuchs in his examination of the company statistics portion of the 1954 Census of Manufactures. Fuchs found that value added per employee in conglomerates exceeded that in single-establisment companies by 28 percent. It exceeded that in multi-unit, single-industry companies by 11 percent. Conglomerates paid their employees 9 percent more than single-unit firms and 4 percent more than multi-unit, single-industry firms.[6] On average, conglomerates produced 22 percent more with each worker than single-industry firms and paid their workers 7 percent more in 1954 (see table 8).

An analysis of the 1963 Census of Manufactures enterprise statistics shows even greater productivity and pay rates in conglomerates, in relation to single-unit and multi-unit, single-industry companies, than in 1954. The amount by which value added per employee in conglomerates exceeded value added in single-unit firms rose from 28 percent in 1954 to 38 percent in 1963. Value added per employee in conglomerates rose from 11 percent to 15 percent more than in multi-unit, single-industry firms between 1954 and 1963. Pay rates in conglomerates rose from 9 percent more than in single-unit firms in 1954 to 13 percent more in 1963. Wage rates in conglomerates rose from 7 percent more than in single-industry firms in 1954 to 11 percent more in 1963 (see table 8).

This disequilibrium in 1963 may have been one of the more important reasons for the conglomerate merger wave of the 1960s. Why the increase in the disequilibrium occurred, between 1954 and 1963, we do not know. Whatever the reason, the rise in conglomeration in the 1960s brought the economy back toward a structural equilibrium between 1963 and 1972. Value added per employee fell from 30 percent greater in conglomerates than in single-industry firms in 1963 to 17 percent greater in 1972 (measured by arithmetic means) as a result of the reallocation of resources from single-industry to multi-industry firms (see table 8). This suggests that it was the less efficient single-industry firms that conglomerates acquired. It was in these that conglomerates could bring about improvements in output per employee.

6. Victor R. Fuchs, "Integration, Concentration, and Profits in Manufacturing Industries," *Quarterly Journal of Economics*, vol. 75 (May 1961), p. 281. According to data provided in Willard L. Thorp, Walter F. Crowder et al., *The Structure of Industry*, Temporary National Economic Committee, monograph no. 27 (1941), pp. 161, 211, multi-industry firms paid annual wages 23.8 percent higher than single-industry firms in 1937.

TABLE 8

Value Added and Wages per Employee in Conglomerate Firms and Single-Industry Firms, 1954–1972

Ratio of Conglomerate Firm Employee Productivity (or Wage) to Single-Industry Firm Employee Productivity (or Wage)	Number of Enterprise Industries in Each Range of Employee Productivity Ratios			Number of Enterprise Industries in Each Range of Wage Rate Ratios		
	1954	1963	1972	1954	1963	1972
2.00 and over	1	4	1	—	—	—
1.90–1.99	2	3	1	—	—	—
1.80–1.89	—	2	—	—	—	—
1.70–1.79	1	3	3	—	—	1
1.60–1.69	3	2	2	1	3	2
1.50–1.59	1	5	1	—	3	5
1.40–1.49	6	6	6	8	13	8
1.30–1.39	7	13	7	22	38	28
1.20–1.29	14	14	12	27	36	32
1.10–1.19	19	31	23	18	14	14
1.00–1.09	13	16	11	2	—	1
0.90–0.99	7	6	14	—	—	—
0.80–0.89	4	2	8	—	—	—
0.70–0.79	—	—	2	—	—	—
Total number of industries	78	107	91	78	107	91
Median	1.15	1.19	1.13	1.07	1.10	1.09
Mean	1.22	1.30	1.17	1.07	1.11	1.10

NOTE: Dashes indicate 0.
SOURCES: Bureau of the Census, *Enterprise Statistics: 1963*, pt. 1, *General Report on Industrial Organization* (1968), table 5A; *Enterprise Statistics* (1977), table 2.

In this respect, the conglomerate merger wave of the 1960s may have been similar to the horizontal mergers of the 1930s and 1940s. Most of the firms acquired in those horizontal mergers had suboptimal capacity.[7] Combining their assets by merger formed firms with a larger, more economic scale of operation. These mergers achieved efficiencies without creating excess capacity and driving some firms of less than optimum size into bankruptcy or voluntary liquidation—a more costly way of increasing productivity.

Sources of Conglomerate Efficiency

The sources of the greater productivity of employees of conglomerates have not been determined. Perhaps the joint use of warehouses, delivery trucks, and sales forces and the use of pool car shipments result in economies in some product-extension mergers.[8] Perhaps conglomerates replace incompetent managers in acquired firms. Perhaps they are quicker to take action when performance in a division lags. Perhaps they move more rapidly than single-industry companies to discontinue inefficient or unproductive operations and to put their employees and capital to more productive uses. Perhaps they do not throw good money after bad.[9] Perhaps their ability to raise capital at less cost than smaller or less diversified firms enables them to use more capital-intensive technology. Perhaps their internal capital markets in a day of shortened product-life cycles work more efficiently than impersonal capital markets.[10]

The opportunity to use an internal capital market rather than go to external sources can be crucial when financing is necessary to make use of proprietary information. A firm seeking capital from outside the company to apply new technology developed in its research department may have to disclose some of the informaton on its new development to obtain funds. But disclosing the information may dis-

7. Leonard Weiss, "An Evaluation of Mergers in Six Industries," *Review of Economics and Statistics,* vol. 47 (May 1965), p. 172.

8. James Ferguson suggests that product-extension mergers, where the products are sold to the same customers, may result in economies by using the same sales force, warehouses, and other facilities in distribution and marketing. Clorox and S.O.S. were sold through brokers before their acquisition by Procter and Gamble and by General Foods. After acquisition, they were sold by the existing sales force of the acquirers. "Anticompetitive Effects of the FTC's Attack on Product-Extension Mergers," *St. John's Law Review,* vol. 44 (Spring 1970), p. 399.

9. Henry G. Grabowski and Dennis Mueller, "Life Cycle Effects of Corporate Returns on Retentions," *Review of Economics and Statistics,* vol. 57 (November 1975).

10. For a discussion of managerial techniques in financial, managerial, and concentric conglomerates, see J. Fred Weston, *Industrial Concentration, Mergers, and Growth* (Washington, D.C.: U.S. Department of Commerce, 1980).

sipate some of its value since competitors may, as a consequence, come into the market more quickly:

> The subsidiaries of a conglomerate can disclose proprietary information to corporate headquarters, and thus the corporation can allocate its capital based on a full information set. . . . This is . . . why the internal capital market of a large firm may be a more efficient allocator of capital than the external capital market.[11]

Richard Nelson, in his paper "The Simple Economics of Basic Scientific Research," concluded that conglomerate firms obtain a better return on their investments in research and development because they "have their fingers in many pies." Their interests in many fields enable them to produce and market a larger proportion of the unexpected inventions that occur in their research efforts, and they make more use of basic research. According to Nelson:

> A broad technological base insures that, whatever direction the path of research may take, the results are likely to be of value to the sponsoring firm. . . . It is not just the size of the companies that makes it worthwhile for them to engage in basic research. Rather it is their broad technological base, the wide range of products they produce or will be willing to produce if their research efforts open possibilities. . . . Strangely enough, economists have tended to see little economic justification for giant firms not built on economies of scale. Yet it is the many-product giants, not the single-product giants, which have been most technologically dynamic.[12]

Conglomerates, by increasing their size through their acquisitions, may also economize in staff functions. A study by Peter Pashigian of the 284 respondents (most of them conglomerates) to a questionnaire on legal costs sent to the leading 500 industrial firms found a strong inverse relationship between legal costs per million dollars of sales and size (see table 9). If the average cost of other staff functions per dollar of sales drops anywhere near as rapidly as legal

11. Jay R. Ritter, "Innovation and Communications: Signaling with Partial Disclosure" (Paper presented at the Workshop in Applied Price Theory, University of Chicago, March 4, 1980).

12. Richard R. Nelson, "The Simple Economics of Basic Research," *Journal of Political Economy*, vol. 67 (June 1959), p. 302. See also, Albert N. Link and James E. Long, "The Simple Economics of Basic Scientific Research: A Test of Nelson's Diversification Hypothesis," *Journal of Industrial Economics*, vol. 30, no. 1 (September 1981), pp. 105–9.

TABLE 9

Legal Costs per Million Dollars
of Sales, by Firm Size

Average Sales of Firms ($ millions)	Average Legal Costs per $1 million of Sales (dollars)
300	2,227
750	1,527
1,000	1,085
2,000 and over	440

Source: B. Peter Pashigian, "The Legal Costs of Firms: Prevention versus Legal Defense" (Paper presented at the Law and Economics Workshop, University of Chicago, May 20, 1980).

costs, these economies may be a factor in the willingness of conglomerates to pay substantial premiums for their acquistions.[13] They make it possible to earn a normal return on these investments despite the large premiums paid.

Perhaps, as Harold Geneen, former president of International Telephone and Telegraph, explained, a conglomerate "has numerous individual specialists and experienced managers in many fields, and . . . the very untraditional outlook such a company brings to an industry is the key to innovation and new progress."[14] When Mobil acquired Montgomery Ward, it placed its own credit management specialists in Ward's troubled credit operation and lent real estate experts and location specialists from its filling-station-location group to Ward's store-location group. It also applied its retailing expertise and its purchasing know-how to Ward's operation. The superior management and staff of a firm may enable it to improve operations in other firms lacking such management and such staffs.[15]

---

13. Ferguson, in his analysis of the Procter and Gamble merger with Clorox and the General Foods merger with S.O.S., concludes, "Apparently, the merger gave the acquired firms access to the expertise of marketing men in the acquiring firms. . . . It is also possible since both acquiring firms devoted million of dollars to sales promotion activites, that economies of size in these activities were made available to the acquired firms." "Anticompetitive Effects," p. 399.

14. Harold S. Geneen, "Conglomerates: A Businessman's View," *St. John's Law Review*, vol. 44 (Spring 1970), p. 725.

15. Although companies needing management assistance may call on consultants, anyone providing consulting services can relate many stories of how often advice suggesting obviously productive possible improvements is disregarded. The ability to enforce the adoption of advice is necessary as well as the advice itself.

The "Consumption" of Capital by Acquirers

Opponents of the merger movement frequently argue that the use of borrowings (for example, by du Pont to acquire Conoco or by Mobil to acquire General Crude Oil) would do more for the nation if used by acquirers to build new plant, to do more innovating, or to find new oil rather than to acquire already discovered oil and already built plants. They believe that the use of capital for acquisitions denies capital to real capital formation.

The simple correlation of assets acquired by manufacturing and mining firms with spending on the creation of new assets is very high. The correlation coefficient is 0.85. The acquisition of old and new assets is not a process in which spending on old assets diverts capital from the creation of new assets. An increase in the demand for old assets encourages the creation of new assets. We recognize this in the case of housing yet do not apply the same reasoning to other assets. That an increase in the demand for old houses will increase the demand for new houses is a part of the conventional wisdom. The same principle applies to other assets.

The fact that a firm finds it cheaper to buy already discovered oil than to engage in discovery itself or add to its current discovery effort simply says that it is less efficient at discovery than others or that the added effort would be less efficient.[16] By buying already discovered oil, it increases the demand for discovered oil. Those who *have* discovered oil and are more efficient in discovery sell their reserves and are provided with the capital to engage in additional discovery. Those who earlier invested in companies that discovered oil are, when their companies are acquired, provided with the capital to invest in more discoveries of oil. The result is additional investment in new discovery whether the capital is invested directly by a Mobil or indirectly by its purchase of already discovered reserves. Even if those who sell their positions in already discovered oil do not themselves reinvest in more discovery, others are encouraged to invest by the demand for discovered oil.

To put this another way, an acquisition does not consume the real resources required for the creation of new assets. The purchase of one company by another simply transfers title. It does not divert the real resources used to create new assets to noncreative uses. If anything,

---

16. At the time Mobil made its $5.1 billion bid for Marathon, it was already spending nearly $4 billion a year for its capital and exploration budget. It obviously felt that adding to its exploration budget would do less to increase its reserves than the purchase of Marathon. Paul Blustein, "Mobil's Bid for Marathon Reflects Lessons from Conoco Offer, Urge to Gain Reserves," *Wall Street Journal*, November 4, 1981.

acquisitions of existing assets attract additional real resources into creating more new real assets. Remember the correlation between the purchase of existing assets and the creation of new assets.

When firms choose to buy existing assets, such as already discovered oil, where that is cheaper than discovering their own, the process of creating new assets, such as newly discovered oil, is made more efficient. Those who are most efficient at discovery will engage in it and sell to those who are less efficient. To bar such acquisitions will make the discovery process less efficient and reduce the amount of oil discovered both for this reason and because of the forced reduction in the demand for already discovered oil.

Conclusion

Whether conglomerates increase the efficiency of the American economy is a question that has baffled many observers. How can putting cigarettes and Hawaiian Punch under one corporate umbrella have any startling effects on efficiency? Whether or not the answer is apparent to the naked eye is irrelevant. There may be as many different reasons for an increase in efficiency resulting from conglomerate mergers as there are efficient mergers, not one or a few answers applicable to a wide variety of cases. For this reason, no single answer can be discovered.[17] There have been and will continue to be instances in which it is clear, after the fact, that a merger was a mistake. But it should be even clearer that to prevent mistakes government would have to prevent people from making decisions. If our capital, labor, material, and product markets function competitively, they will accord rewards to those that are efficient and losses to those that are not.

Many acquisitions have been mistakes. Some conglomerates overreached themselves. Some large firms overexpanded. But the market cured this. Would-be conglomerates that failed to manage acquired assets as competently as others, as apparently was the case at Whittaker Corporation and Ling-Temco-Vought, were forced to disgorge some of their acquisitions and reorganize their operations to stay alive. American Brands, W. R. Grace, and other conglomerates have sold portions of their acquisitions to finance their activities and to confine their operations to what they can manage well. As William G. Shepherd found: "Many mergers are divestitures rather than a combination

17. "That there is no general theory of productive efficiency gains suggests that most efficiency gains are not routine or regular. Efficiencies might originate in technical scale economies, any of the corporate functions (finance, production, marketing research, etc.), product quality and image, transaction costs, or the quality of managerial decision making." John R. Carter, "Actual Potential Entry under Section 7 of the Clayton Act," *Virginia Law Review*, vol. 66, no. 8 (December 1980), p. 1492, n. 27.

of two free-standing companies. Such selling off of branches rose in 1975 to 54 percent of all acquisitions (by number), up from 11 percent in 1967 and 39 percent in 1973."[18]

What is surprising is that evidence of greater relative efficiency in conglomerates shows so strongly in the data (table 8). It would not do so if the economy were in a long-run, static structural equilibrium. With full adjustment to tastes, resources, and technology, wage rates and productivity would be no higher in multi-industry than in single-industry firms. Only to the extent that capital is less expensive to conglomerates would we see higher output per labor-hour in conglomerates when the economy is at or near a secular equilibrium. In this situation, we would also see lower rates of return in the multi-industry firms.

The data showing larger than normal disparities in value added per employee hour in different enterprises, as in 1963, indicate a disequilibrium that could be expected to produce the structural re-arrangements of the sort seen in the latter 1960s. A disequilibrium means that resources are not being allocated to their most productive uses. Conglomerates, by moving employees and capital from less to more productive applications (perhaps by simply improving the management of those resources in their current use), contributed to growth and to improvements in the level of living.

On average, acquirers improved asset management, provided stockholders of poorly managed firms with an improvement in the value of their holdings, reallocated capital and labor from less to more productive uses, and improved the economic health of the country. They brought us closer to a long-run, efficient equilibrium in the allocation of resources, despite the continuing movement of the equilibrium position.

18. William G. Shepherd, *The Economics of Industrial Organization* (Englewood Cliffs, N.J.: Prentice-Hall, 1979), p. 163.

4
Mergers and
Conglomerate Power

Some recent arrivals on the Big Fifty list, such as Gulf and Western, International Telephone, and Tenneco, got there by acquiring dozens of diverse firms and divisions sold by other firms. They are conglomerates—or, as they prefer to call themselves, multi-industry or multimarket companies.[1] Harmful effects are alleged to stem from their size. Sinister motives are said to underlie their diversification. Fears that conglomerates will engage in reciprocal arrangements—transactions in which the conglomerate coerces a seller by saying to him, "I will buy your product only if you buy mine"—are raised. It is also suggested that these multimarketers use cross-subsidization to grow larger and to dominate markets in which their divisions operate. Presumably they subsidize predatory activity by some divisions with the profits of other divisions.

The desire to present the conglomerate corporation as a destructive or exploitive economic organism often leads to a Jekyll and Hyde caricature in which the pitiless competitive instincts of one minute are replaced by the collusive, parasitic impulses of the next. Con-

---

1. Practically all the 200 largest manufacturing corporations of 1968 were widely diversified. Those not labeled conglomerates differed from those that were only because they had not been heavily engaged in merger or acquisition activity in the postwar period. In addition, they generally had a much larger share, frequently more than 50 percent, of their business concentrated in one industry. Only 16 of the 200 operated in fewer than six four-digit industries, and only three produced in fewer than six five-digit product classes. Nearly three-quarters (146) of the 200 operated in eleven or more four-digit industries, and 90 percent (181) produced in eleven or more five-digit product classes. Federal Trade Commission, Bureau of Economics, *Economic Report on Corporate Mergers* (1969), p. 233.

Conglomerates are simply spectacular examples of diversification. Not only are "most large firms diversified to some extent; the degree of diversification has increased significantly from 1950 to 1968. Thus, the conglomerates are not unique, but are merely extreme examples of a trend that has occurred in manufacturing generally." Staff Report to the Federal Trade Commission, *Conglomerate Merger Performance: An Empirical Analysis of Nine Corporations* (November 1972), p. 85.

glomerates *might* entrench their acquisitions in their markets by predatory cross-subsidization, or they *might* profit from mutual competitive forbearance.

Potential Predatory Pricing

The cross-subsidization argument is another version of the predatory pricing fear. That is, it assumes that one of the divisions of a conglomerate *might* price below cost, financing this money-losing endeavor with profits earned in other divisions, to drive out competitors. Once it drives competitors from the field, the division could, it is asserted, raise its price to monopoly levels, recouping its losses with interest and more.

Although this possibility has gained adherents in Washington and in the courts—despite the fact that antitrust laws can be applied by the government and that injured competitors can sue for treble damages in such cases—hardly an economist specializing in industrial organization believes that this strategy is feasible or profitable.[2] James Lorie and Paul Halpern observe, "In the long run, and in the absence of effective barriers to entry, it seems impossible to maintain an effective monopoly by a temporarily superior capacity to lose money."[3] Professor David Kamerschen tells us:

> I think there is something of a consensus among industrial organization economists that true predation is very unusual, probably illogical, and not a serious social problem in the U.S. The following quotations from respected scholars in this area should suffice to illustrate this consensus: (1) Elzinga . . . "Predatory price cutting, given its unlikely occurrence and visual similarity to healthy business rivalry, should be well down the priority list of the antitrust authorities"; (2) Dewey . . . "From the foregoing remarks, it also follows that predatory price-cutting constitutes a minor threat to competition"; (3) Scherer . . . "Distinguishing price cutting with

2. Frank H. Easterbrook, "Predatory Strategies and Counterstrategies," *University of Chicago Law Review*, vol. 48, no. 2 (Spring 1981), pp. 283–337; John S. McGee, "Predatory Price Cutting: The Standard Oil (N.J.) Case," *Journal of Law and Economics*, vol. 1 (October 1958); Roland H. Koller II, "The Myth of Predatory Pricing: An Empirical Study" in Yale Brozen, ed., *The Competitive Economy: Selected Readings* (Morristown, N.J.: General Learning Press, 1975); Wayne A. Leeman, "The Limitations of Local Price-Cutting as a Barrier to Entry," *Journal of Political Economy*, vol. 64, no. 4 (August 1956); Bjarke Fog, *Industrial Pricing Policies* (Amsterdam: North-Holland, 1960), pp. 147–51; and Morris A. Adelman, *A & P: A Study in Price-Cost Behavior and Public Policy* (Cambridge: Harvard University Press, 1959), p. 14.

3. James H. Lorie and Paul Halpern, "Conglomerates: The Rhetoric and the Evidence," *Journal of Law and Economics*, vol. 13, no. 1 (April 1970), p. 156.

predatory intent from price cutting in good faith to meet tough local competition is singularly difficult . . . . It is fair to say that the predatory pricing doctrine is one of the shakiest pillars of existing antimerger law. Its absence would not be mourned by lovers of competition and/or logic."; and (4) Scherer . . . "in actual situations the line between meeting competition and destroying it is seldom sharp, since a great deal depends upon intent, which is hard to pin down." The legal profession seems equally outspoken as to how threatening a "clog on competition" is predation, arguing that the dangers of predation are few in principle, unlikely in occurrence, and speculative in demonstration.[4]

Speaking directly on the issue of the likelihood of predatory pricing as a consequence of conglomerate mergers, Donald Turner, a former head of the Antitrust Division, notes that

> the belief that predatory pricing is a likely consequence of conglomerate size, and hence of conglomerate merger, is wholly unverified by any careful studies; research and analysis suggest that in all likelihood this belief is just wrong.
>
> To sum up predatory pricing seems so improbable a consequence of conglomerate acquisitions that it deserves little weight in formulating antimerger rules based on prospective effects.[5]

The Bureau of Economics of the Federal Trade Commission treated the prospect of cross-subsidized predatory activity by conglomerates with undisguised skepticism after engaging in a detailed study of conglomerate behavior and performance. In its report on its survey of nine large conglomerates, it states that it found no evidence of predatory behavior nor could it find "any rational incentive for them to do so." It says:

> It should be noted that in calculating the returns from a predatory pricing strategy, a time discount factor would have to be applied to the expected monopoly return. The "deep pocket" losses would occur in the present, whereas the monopoly returns would begin at some distant point in the

---

4. David R. Kamerschen, "Predatory Pricing, Vertical Integration, and Market Foreclosure: The Case of Ready Mix Concrete in Memphis," *Industrial Organization Review*, vol. 2, no. 3 (1974), p. 144, n. 12, citing Kenneth Elzinga, "Predatory Pricing: The Case of the Gunpowder Trust," *Journal of Law and Economics*, vol. 13, no. 1 (April 1970), p. 240; Donald Dewey, "Competitive Policy and National Goals: The Doubtful Relevance of Antitrust" in Almarin Phillips, ed., *Perspectives on Antitrust Policy* (Princeton, N.J.: Princeton University Press, 1965), p. 81; and Frederic M. Scherer, *Industrial Market Structure and Economic Performance* (Chicago: Rand McNally, 1970), pp. 484; 202.

5. Donald F. Turner, "Conglomerate Mergers and Section 7 of the Clayton Act," *Harvard Law Review*, vol. 78, no. 7 (May 1965), pp. 1339–40, 1346.

future, perhaps ten years hence. Only when the losses were small or of short duration, or the monopoly profits very large, would such a strategy be economically rational for a conglomerate. In addition, a predatory strategy presumes that there are significant entry barriers in the market where the conglomerate is attempting to eliminate smaller rivals. Otherwise, new firms would enter after prices were raised and the conglomerate would not be able to reap monopoly profits.[6]

Similarly, the Presidential Task Force on Productivity and Competition stated:

> There is now an impressive body of literature arguing the improbability that a profit maximizing seller, even one with monopoly power, would or could use below-cost selling to monopolize additional markets. Yet . . . the alleged danger of predatory pricing remains a principal prop of [the FTC] vertical and conglomerate antimerger cases.[7]

The unlikelihood of predatory pricing was cogently demonstrated by Earle Birdzell. The considerations he lists that would have to be taken into account in preparing a business plan for taking over an industry through predatory pricing show that such a plan would be extraordinarily expensive.[8] The improbability of predatory pricing is confirmed by its rarity.[9]

The direct evidence on the trends in market share of conglomerate acquisitions after merger demonstrates that neither entrenchment nor predatory pricing is a common tactic (or else conglomerates were remarkably inept in their use of predatory pricing).

> The post-acquisition changes in market positions acquired by conglomerates from 1963 to 1969 were predominantly decreases. . . . After the massive merger activity of the 1960s, the market share of the conglomerate firm in 1969 was less than 5 percent in 82.4 percent of the five-digit product classes in which they operated.[10]

6. Staff Report to the Federal Trade Commission, *Conglomerate Merger Performance*, p. 4.

7. "Report of the Task Force on Productivity and Competition," *Congressional Record*, vol. 115 (June 16, 1969), p. 6475.

8. L. Earle Birdzell, "The Conglomerates: A Neighbor's View," *St. John's Law Review*, vol. 44 (Spring 1970), pp. 306–8.

9. Joel Davidow, "Conglomerate Concentration and Section Seven: The Limitations of the Antimerger Act," *Columbia Law Review*, vol. 68 (November 1968), p. 1256. See also Turner, "Conglomerate Mergers," pp. 1340, 1346.

10. J. Fred Weston, "The FTC Staff's Economic Report on Conglomerate Merger Performance," *Bell Journal of Economics and Management Science*, vol. 4, no. 2 (Autumn 1973), p. 685.

It should be added that the fact that "the post-acquisition changes in market positions acquired by conglomerates from 1963 to 1969 were predominantly decreases" is no surprise. Most of the acquisitions of the conglomerates were firms that had been performing poorly. Chapter 3 lists, among the sources of inefficiency in the acquired firms, the "throwing of good money after bad." A source of conglomerate efficiency is the avoidance of such action. The internal capital markets within conglomerates provide more productive alternatives for resources in many instances, particularly when the acquired company's industry is overexpanded.

Potential Reciprocity

Reciprocity is an even weaker pillar of antitrust than predatory pricing. Wesley Liebeler suggests that any cartel laying down rules to prevent secret, difficult-to-detect price cuts that cheat on the cartel's price policy would forbid purchases by any member of the cartel from its customers. If such purchases could be made and were allowed, it would be simple for any member to overpay a customer for supplies bought from the customer as a way of secretly shading the cartel price to obtain business.[11]

The lower price would not appear on any invoice, and inspection of the cartel member's books would show no violation of the cartel agreement. Liebeler goes on to suggest that if the antitrust agencies had stumbled across a reciprocity ban by a price-colluding group, it would have become antitrust doctrine to forbid the *prevention* of reciprocal purchases. Yet the antitrust agencies moved to forbid LTV's acquisition of Jones and Laughlin on the ground that it enhanced the possibility of reciprocal dealing, and the FTC forced Consolidated Foods to divest itself of Gentry because of reciprocal dealing.

Reciprocal dealing is either a procompetitive[12] or an innocent practice.[13] In one instance it was a method of exporting profits from a division where they would be subject to renegotiation on defense

11. Wesley J. Liebeler, remarks at the Conference on Antitrust at the Center for Law and Economics, University of Miami, December 1, 1978.

12. "If this interpretation of Consolidated Foods is correct, reciprocity appears to have had a profoundly pro-competitive effect." Wesley J. Liebeler, "The Emperor's New Clothes: Why Is Reciprocity Anticompetitive?" *St. John's Law Review,* vol. 44 (Spring 1970), p. 558.

13. "Reciprocal buying . . . might, of course, lead to greater efficiency (for example by reducing marketing costs) or it might lead to inefficiency. If this practice leads to inefficiency, there is no reason why the conglomerate should adopt it (since it would reduce its overall profits)." Ronald Coase, "Working Paper II: The Conglomerate Merger" (for the Presidential Task Force on Productivity and Competition), *Antitrust Law and Economics Review,* vol. 2 (Spring 1969), p. 45.

contracts to a division where they would be sheltered. There is no case where reciprocity has been an anticompetitive device to my knowledge. It was most extensively used by railroads unable to compete for business by offering a lower rate because of the price *floors* set by the Interstate Commerce Commission. Given the restrictions on methods of competing, railroads commonly resorted to offering to buy supplies from potential customers if they would purchase the railroad's services.[14] Other firms wishing to cut prices secretly have engaged in similar reciprocal deals to disguise a price cut.

Instead of being imposed as a condition for purchase, as usually argued by the antitrust agencies, reciprocal dealing is ordinarily a sales device. A seller offers to buy from his prospective customer to persuade him to purchase. It has the same competitive effect as an offer of generous credit terms, quick delivery, payment of transportation charges, provision of display or shelf-stocking service, etc.

Secret, discriminatory price cutting works to undermine collusion.[15] It provides a method of competing when the explicit price is fixed. It also helps move a competitive industry more quickly to a new, long-run, lower-price equilibrium.[16] Since reciprocal dealing is a way of granting price concessions that would not be granted if such concessions had to be offered openly, it would seem that we should welcome additional possibilities for reciprocal dealing. While this might be a reason for favoring conglomerate mergers rather than disapproving of them, it turns out that conglomeration evidently does not increase the amount of reciprocal dealing.[17] Modern methods of managing multi-industry firms, with division managers judged by divisional profit performance, militate against the use of reciprocal dealing by conglomerates to any greater extent than by single-industry firms.[18]

14. "The most striking reciprocity cases go back to the 1930s and arise out of efforts to break legally regulated monopoly prices." Birdzell, "The Conglomerates," p. 312.

15. George Stigler, "A Theory of Oligopoly," *Journal of Political Economy*, vol. 72, no. 1 (February 1964), reprinted in George J. Stigler, *The Organization of Industry* (Homewood, Ill.: Richard D. Irwin, 1968); and John S. McGee, "Price Discrimination and Competitive Effects: The Standard Oil of Indiana Case," *University of Chicago Law Review*, vol. 23 (1956), p. 401.

16. Brozen, *The Competitive Economy*, p. 379.

17. "Nor is the reciprocity argument supported by the data. Among the functions analyzed to determine the extent to which their administration in an acquired firm was changed after acquisition, the least number of changes was observed in purchasing— about 4 percent of the acquisitions covered." Weston, "FTC Staff's Report," p. 686.

18. Jesse Markham, *Conglomerate Enterprise and Public Policy* (Boston: Graduate School of Business Administration, Harvard University, 1973). See also, Jules Backman, "Conglomerate Mergers and Competition," *St. John's Law Review*, vol. 44 (Spring 1970), pp. 99–100.

Entrenchment and Potential Mutual Forbearance

The "entrenchment" argument against conglomerate acquisitions, used recently by the Antitrust Division in its attempt to stop the merger of Occidental and Mead, is the opposite of the "competitive forbearance" argument invented by Corwin Edwards. He suggested, without any evidence, that when large firms face each other in many markets, "there is an incentive to live and let live, to cultivate a cooperative spirit, and to recognize priorities of interest in the hope of reciprocal recognition."[19] Yet the division argued against Occidental Petroleum's acquisition of Mead on the ground that Occidental would entrench Mead's position in the paper industry by expanding its business. Entrenchment was used in this case as another name for the "deep pockets" argument. Occidental would, said the division, provide Mead with additional capacity for increasing sales to current customers and for winning additional customers.[20] This hardly smacks of competitive forbearance.[21]

Implicitly, the entrenchment argument suggests that there are advantages to size that will automatically accrue to any large company moving into a market. It will acquire an ever-increasing share of that market by taking business from existing firms. If there are such important and uniform advantages of size across industries, we should capitalize on these advantages to the fullest extent by moving large corporations into every industry. That would bring the economies of size to sellers with small market shares and keep a larger number of sellers alive in each market.

The evidence does not suggest such uniform and automatic advantages in every industry, however. Michael Gort's study of 111 diversified firms showed that these firms continued to occupy only a minor share of most markets many years after entry.[22] The FTC's Bureau of Economics in a detailed study of nine conglomerates came to the same conclusion. In the language of the report: "Looking at leading positions—market shares over 10 percent—increases and decreases

19. Corwin Edwards, "Conglomerate Bigness as a Source of Power," in National Bureau of Economic Research, *Business Concentration and Price Policy* (Princeton, N.J.: Princeton University Press, 1955), p. 335.

20. "Government Widens Trust Suit Opposing Occidental Petroleum Bid for Mead Corp.," *Wall Street Journal*, October 26, 1978.

21. Weston points out that the evidence on the postacquisition fate of market positions acquired by conglomerates does not square with the competitive forbearance hypothesis. "In 98 percent of the acquisitions, a change in market position took place—either an increase or decrease. This high frequency of changes in market share positions does not support the mutual forbearance theory." Weston, "FTC Staff's Report," p. 686.

22. Michael Gort, *Diversification and Integration in American Industry* (Princeton, N.J.: Princeton University Press, 1963).

after acquisition were evenly matched. The conclusion to be drawn . . . is that there is no systematic tendency for market shares either to increase or decrease after acquisition. This is true both for 'toehold' and for leading positions."[23]

As was pointed out in chapter 2, the largest firms in many industries have frequently suffered dramatic drops in their share of the markets in which they operate. If a large share of an industry's output or large size entrenches a company in its leading position, these dramatic decreases in concentration ratios and market shares would not have occurred (see tables 5, 6, and 7).

Conclusion

Section 7 of the Clayton Act forbids mergers where the effect "may be substantially to lessen competition, or tend to create a monopoly." In the leading antitrust case in which a conglomerate merger was ruled illegal (Procter and Gamble–Clorox), the "may" was stretched beyond any reasonable bounds to include all possible actions.[24] A course of action is not likely or probable when (1) the actual actions taken are opposite to those supposed to be possible and (2) the possible action would be illogical.

In the Procter and Gamble–Clorox merger, the Federal Trade Commission's case rested, in part, on the possible use of Procter and Gamble's "deep pocket" (its large size in relation to the size of other producers of liquid bleach) and the discounts it received for increased use of network television. The latter was irrelevant since only "spot" television was used by Procter and Gamble, and by Clorox before the merger, to advertise Clorox liquid bleach. Network discounts do not apply to spot commercials. The deep-pocket argument was equally irrelevant for these reasons:

1. If it paid to engage in predatory activity to obtain a monopoly, Clorox was as capable as Procter and Gamble of supporting the financing of the activity (it was more than three times the size of its nearest competitor in the nation, and in some regions it was ten times the size of its nearest competitor).[25]

23. Staff Report to the Federal Trade Commission, *Conglomerate Merger Performance*, p. 84.

24. Lee Loevinger, "How to Succeed in Business without Being Tried—the Potentiality of Antitrust Prosecution," *Arizona Law Review*, vol. 12, no. 3 (Fall 1970), pp. 451–52. The court of appeals reversed the FTC's finding of illegality in Procter and Gamble–Clorox because it had been based on "treacherous conjecture, mere possibility and suspicion." The Supreme Court, however, ruled that the evidence was adequate and upheld the commission.

25. "The notion that a large firm will lose money because it can afford to do so, puts

2. Predatory activity would have been foolish in the liquid bleach industry since entry barriers were nonexistent. Any attempt to recoup the losses from predation would have been met with nearly instant entry of new competitors and expansion of existing competitors, of whom there were 200 at the time of the merger and in the subsequent years before the case reached the Supreme Court.

3. Increased advertising and promotion of bleach by Procter and Gamble financed out of its deep pocket did not squeeze out competitors. It created a coattail effect that *increased* the sales of Clorox competitors as well as those of Clorox. The increased sales of Clorox competitors were mentioned in the Court's opinion, but the Court dismissed their relevance on the ground that one could have predicted an opposite result from the merger even though the prediction would be and was wrong.

In another leading antitrust case in which a conglomerate merger was ruled illegal, Consolidated Foods–Gentry, reciprocity was the primary focus of the attack. But, as we have pointed out, reciprocity is not an anticompetitive tactic. It is procompetitive or innocent in its effect. In this instance, it was "profoundly pro-competitive."[26] In a nearly duopolized market, the entry of Consolidated Foods by acquisition of one of the two leading firms ended the neglect of product quality, customer service, and distribution by the other leading firm and led to reduced prices.[27]

The attack on conglomerate mergers apparently has been based on the large size of the acquiring firms and a presumed possible or potential loss of business by competitors (the antitrust doctrine nominally used was the possible effect of a loss of a perceived potential entrant). But size is not illegal, and loss of business by less efficient competitors is what competition is intended to accomplish. The antitrust laws are supposed to favor competition, not prevent it. As the Task Force on Competition and Productivity observed:

> The large conglomerate enterprise . . . almost by definition . . . poses at most a minor threat to competition. . . . If one interprets "elimination of potential competition," "reciprocity," and "foreclosure" as threats to competition, one can always bring and usually win a case against the merger of two large companies, however diverse their

the cart before the horse. They will do no such thing unless there is a dollar to be made eventually; and if there is a dollar to be made, a local concern will be just as keen in seeking it and much less inhibited by fear of the law." Morris A. Adelman, "The Antimerger Act, 1950–1960," *American Economic Review*, vol. 51 (May 1961), pp. 242–43.

26. Liebeler, "The Emperor's New Clothes," p. 558.

27. Ibid.

activities may be. These are often makeweights. The economic threat to competition from reciprocity (reciprocal buying arrangements) is either small or nonexistent: monopoly power in one commodity is not effectively exploited by manipulating the price of an unrelated commodity.[28]

We should add James Ferguson's observation that, where there are economies of size in a market or an industry, "the only way to maintain the existing number of firms in a small firm industry . . . is to permit every firm in the industry to merge with a firm in another market."[29] That would bring the economies of size to sellers who are not the leading firms in their markets, keep a larger number of sellers alive in each market, and thus preserve a larger number of competitors in each. In the absence of such mergers, economies of size will come after a competitive struggle eliminates many sellers and concentrates business in the hands of a few. "Therefore, the FTC reaches exactly the wrong conclusion in attacking these mergers in pursuit of its policy of maintaining existing competitors in these markets."[30]

28. "Report of the Task Force on Productivity and Competition," p. 6475.

29. James Ferguson, "Anticompetitive Effects of the FTC's Attack on Product-Extension Mergers," *St. John's Law Review*, vol. 44 (Spring 1970), p. 395.

30. Ibid.

5
Mergers versus Entry De Novo

One of the arguments advanced against allowing large conglomerates to grow larger by acquisitions does not concern itself primarily with size or aggregate concentration. Instead the issue is the desirability of atomistic market structures—a turn back to the arguments against market concentration.[1] The antitrust authorities have been concerned that a firm making a conglomerate acquisition ceases to be a *potential* competitor when it becomes an actual competitor by acquisition. Their hope, apparently, was that foreclosing diversification by acquisition would lead the would-be acquirer to enter the same industry *de novo* by internal expansion (or if by acquisition, then by no more than a "toehold" acquisition). The premise of this position is a belief that the motive for conglomerate mergers is a desire for diversification into specific lines of business.

Why Conglomerate Mergers Occur

The use of this argument simply demonstrates that the antitrust authorities do not know why conglomerate acquisitions occur. Chief among the many reasons for conglomerate mergers—and the best-substantiated hypothesis—is that conglomerates take advantage of opportunities to acquire poorly managed assets.[2] (On these they earn

1. The arguments against high market concentration, where it exists, and against increases in concentration, where they occur, have been shown in several studies to lack foundation. John S. McGee, *In Defense of Industrial Concentration* (New York: Praeger, 1971); Sam Peltzman, "The Gains and Losses from Industrial Concentration," *Journal of Law and Economics*, vol. 20, no. 2 (October 1977); Harold Demsetz, "Two Systems of Belief about Monopoly," in Harvey Goldschmid, H. Michael Man, and J. Fred Weston, eds., *Industrial Concentration: The New Learning* (Boston: Little, Brown and Co., 1974); John R. Carter, "Collusion, Efficiency, and Antitrust," *Journal of Law and Economics*, vol. 21, no. 2 (October 1978); and Steven Lustgarten, *Industrial Concentration, Productivity Growth, and Consumer Welfare* (Washington, D.C.: American Enterprise Institute, forthcoming). For a review of the literature on both sides of the dispute concerning the effects of high concentration, see Paul A. Pautler, "A Review of the Economic Basis for Broad-Based Horizontal Merger Policy" (working draft, October 1981, Federal Trade Commission).

2. One study tests a "managerial" motive for conglomerate mergers. Managers are

as much as they would be able to make on any other investment. They succeed in making a competitive return on what they invest by managing the assets well.) The Bureau of Economics of the Federal Trade Commission examined the earnings record of eighty-five large firms acquired by nine major conglomerates in the 1960s. It found that

> on the average, the manufacturing firms acquired by the survey firms were significantly less profitable than the average for their industries. . . . The median relative profit rate was 76.5 percent. Thus, the median acquired manufacturing firm was about three-fourths as profitable as the average of other firms in its industry.[3]

The 1955–1976 conglomerate acquisition record, as well as the record of the nine conglomerates studied by the FTC, demonstrates that poorly managed firms predominate among those acquired by

presumed to engage in conglomerate mergers to decrease their employment risk (at the expense of stockholders, though not at the expense of all capital providers since the authors believe that at least some of the wealth stockholders lose is transferred to bondholders). The study cites papers by Peter Dodd ("Merger Proposals, Management Discretion, and Stockholder Wealth" [Working Paper 79–03, Graduate School of Management, University of Rochester, March 1980]) and M. Firth ("Takeovers, Shareholder Returns, and the Theory of the Firm," *Quarterly Journal of Economics*, vol. 94, no. 3 [March 1980]) as demonstrating "a decrease in the stock values of acquiring firms." Yakov Amihud and Baruch Lev, "Risk Reduction as a Managerial Motive for Conglomerate Mergers," *Bell Journal of Economics*, vol. 12, no. 2 (Autumn 1981), pp. 605–6.

It is still primarily the opportunity to acquire a poorly performing firm that motivates specific conglomerate mergers, not the desire to enter a specific industry. A large sample of horizontal and vertical mergers (259 acquisitions in manufacturing and mining) analyzed by Professor Bjorn Eckbo shows gains to the stockholders of *both* the bidding firms and the target firms, which are almost evenly split (on a dollar basis) between the two groups. "Horizontal Mergers, Collusion, and Stockholder Wealth" (working paper, Faculty of Commerce, University of British Columbia, October 1981), p. 31. The Firth paper uses United Kingdom data, and its statistical analysis is not adequately specified. The Dodd paper uses appropriate statistical methods but fails to examine the pre–merger announcement returns. Evidence in other work (unpublished) points to the fact that positive returns are realized by acquirers when they first embark on their merger programs. The returns from later conglomerate acquisitions are anticipated and therefore do not show in postacquisition data except for the first merger in a merger program. The Dodd results appear to be peculiar to the sample and time period chosen. Larger samples and longer time periods do not produce his results.

3. Staff Report to the Federal Trade Commission, *Conglomerate Merger Performance: An Empirical Analysis of Nine Corporations* (November 1972), p. 28. Similar circumstances for acquired firms in West Germany were reported by John J. Cable, J. Palfrey, and J. Runge, "Economic Determinants and Effects of Mergers in West Germany 1964–74," *Zeitschrift fur die Gesamte Staatswissenschaft*, vol. 136, no. 1 (March 1980), p. 230. They found that "acquired companies . . . had been growing at little more than half the rate of their non-merging counterparts. This large difference is statistically significant, and is repeated in eight of the nine individual industries. . . . The acquired firms performed least well [in profitability] of all groups, and significantly less well than their control group." They reported that "horizontal mergers . . . are predominant in the German sample" (p. 239).

FIGURE 3

Earnings of Stockholders of Acquired Firms in Relation to Average Stockholder Earnings in the 480 Business Days Preceding Acquisition Announcement

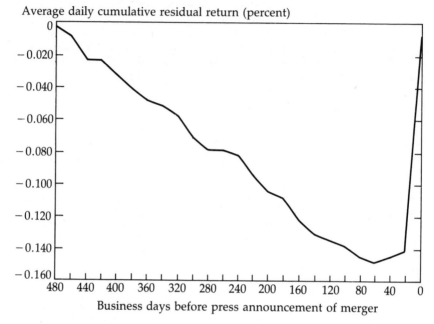

Average daily cumulative residual return (percent)

Business days before press announcement of merger

Source: Paul Asquith, "Mergers and the Market for Acquisitions" (Ph.D. dissertation, Graduate School of Business, University of Chicago, 1980).

merger. Stockholders of the average firm listed on the New York Stock Exchange acquired in the postwar years lost 15 percent on their investment during the 480 business days preceding the news of the acquisition bid compared with the returns to stockholders of the average listed firm (see figure 3). Acquirers paid a competitive price (the value of the firm in competent hands) for their acquisitions (which provided a premium on the price of the stock of the acquired firms that more than made the stockholders of the acquisitions whole). The acquirers earned a competitive return on their acquisitions (see figure 2), demonstrating that (1) they managed them better than they were previously managed and (2) conglomerate takeovers are rational, competitive economic occurrences.[4] Making better use of formerly

4. K. Paul Asquith, "Mergers and the Market for Acquisitions," mimeographed (Graduate School of Business, University of Chicago, 1979). The data provided James H. Lorie and Paul Halpern, "Conglomerates: The Rhetoric and the Evidence," *Journal of Law*

badly managed assets is a social service. It raises productivity, moderates inflation, and should be allowed to proceed.

This evidence suggests that the motive for conglomerate acquisitions is not usually a desire to enter a specific industry.[5] The opportunity to acquire poorly managed assets, to judge by Paul Asquith's findings in his examination of mergers in the post–World War II years, provides the motive for the specific acquisitions made in a majority of cases.[6] The antitrust authorities' "potential entrant" doctrine, however, rests on the premise that foreclosing conglomerate acquisitions will force the conglomerator to enter the field of potential acquisition *de novo*.

It is sometimes argued that the large firms that have become conglomerates did so because their home industries had matured or because they had tax loss carry forwards that would expire unless they acquired profitable firms whose earnings could be sheltered by use of loss carry forwards. While this is true for some conglomerators, it remains that the firms they selected for acquisition were predominantly those that had poor earning experience, not those in industries the conglomerators specifically desired to enter. They may have limited their search to part of the universe of industries but not to a specific industry they would have entered *de novo* or by a toehold acquisition if barred from acquiring the corporations they actually purchased.

The Effect of Conglomerate Mergers on Entry

Even conceding the premises of the antitrust doctrine, it still does not follow that mergers by large conglomerate firms should be barred. It

---

and Economics, vol. 13, no. 1 (April 1970), pp. 149–66, also substantiate this point, although they do not discuss this inference.

5. There are exceptions of course. The recent acquisition of Reliance Electric by Exxon was, according to Exxon statements, a result of a desire to enter the electric motor industry.

6. It has been argued that the poor performance of the stock in the average acquisition is not necessarily an indication of poor management but may be the result of inefficiency in the capital markets in valuing the company. This undervaluation argument is used by Frederic M. Scherer, for example, who says, "The stock market is myopic, and the information that drives it is often flimsy. As a result, some companies tend at any moment in time to be undervalued." *Industrial Market Structure and Market Performance*, 2d ed. (Chicago: Rand McNally, 1980), p. 131. But Asquith found evidence that the firms whose acquisition was attempted were not temporarily undervalued. When merger bids failed, the stockholders of the target firms suffered a loss on average of 8 percent, the same loss they had suffered in the 480 days preceding the announcement of the attempted merger. That is, the stock price *returned* to its preannouncement level. Paul Asquith, "A Two-Event Study of Merger Bids, Market Uncertainty, and Stockholder Returns" (Ph.D. dissertation, Graduate School of Business, University of Chicago, 1980), table 9, p. 32.

can be argued that entry will be decreased by such a bar. The prohibition will be a barrier to entry rather than an encourager of entry *de novo*. That is, it will decrease entry by conglomerates, and it will decrease entry *de novo* by new firms.

If a major portion of conglomerate acquisitions occurs because poor management of assets causes the price of acquired firms to be below their value if well managed, preventing the purchase of these assets will simply decrease the interest of conglomerates in entering the industries where the assets are employed. Stockholders in 93 percent of the firms acquired by conglomerates had returns inferior to those of an average holder of stocks listed on the New York Stock Exchange in the period before the announcement of the merger bid. Eighty percent of all firms acquired by conglomerates suffered relative losses of more than 10 percent. The majority of conglomerate acquisitions evidently consisted of poorly managed firms.[7]

If the earnings experience of the acquired firms' stockholders is, in part, the consequence of the maturation of the industries in which the firms carry on their business, the industry will not be an attractive one to enter *de novo*. With sufficient capacity already in place to depress earnings to a level where a firm earning less than the average in its industry suffers in relation to the average of firms in all industries, entry *de novo* would be a misuse of resources. It would not be attractive since additional capacity placed in such industries would not earn as much, on the average, as alternative investments. It is unrealistic to believe that a conglomerate will try to force its way into an unfamiliar industry with new capacity when there is already sufficient capacity in place to depress average earnings in the industry to the level of the cost of capital.

Some of the acquired firms whose stockholders suffered losses may be in industries in which earnings are attractive, but they are likely to be only a small proportion of such firms. For them to produce relative losses for their stockholders, their managements have to be grossly inadequate. In such a case, the argument for allowing their acquisition by other firms is even more compelling, even at the price of precluding an entry *de novo*.

The inefficiency of the former management of an acquired firm does not necessarily lie in how poorly it managed production or marketing or employee relations. It may simply have consisted of not

7. See Asquith, "Market for Acquisitions." Asquith examined all NYSE firms, other than railroads, acquired by other NYSE firms between 1955 and 1976. Of the 286 mergers in his universe, 43 were horizontal and 22 vertical. The rest were conglomerate. The horizontal and vertical acquisitions did not display poor performance on average. Since the average loss to stockholders of all acquisitions was 15 percent, the losses of stockholders of the firms acquired in conglomerate mergers were approximately 20 percent.

knowing enough to stop throwing good money after bad. If a firm's industry was mature or had begun to decline, continuing to invest in such an industry wasted resources. Borrowings from stockholders in the form of retained earnings or depreciation did not earn enough to maintain the value of the firm's assets and caused the value of the shareholders' assets to decline. Nor was this a service to buyers in general, who obviously preferred the product of alternative investments. Their unwillingness to buy the products of the firm at a price that would yield as good a return as the product of alternative projects demonstrates this.

In fact, it is on exactly this point that those directing conglomerates have displayed good management. Examining a sample of firms that engaged in multiple mergers in the 1960s, Fred Weston and S. K. Mansinghka found that these firms raised the ratio of earnings before interest and taxes to total assets from 8.7 percent in 1958 (compared with 16.7 percent in a control sample) to 15.1 percent in 1968 (compared with 15.6 percent in the control group).[8] These multiple-merger firms obviously were based in overexpanded industries. Instead of throwing good money after bad, they proceeded to allocate resources to more productive uses than could be found in their home industries. Michael Gort's work analyzing the sources of growth for the period 1967 to 1977 in the 100 largest nonoil companies confirms the slower growth of the home industries of these firms. If they had not been or become conglomerates and had simply grown at the same rates as their home two-digit industries, their share of manufacturing sales and assets would have been below what they actually attained.[9]

A portion of the acquisitions of conglomerates consists of firms whose stockholders have suffered no losses. These cannot be categorized as having been inefficiently managed. It could be argued that there is, in this case, an intent to enter a specific industry or to acquire the facilities of a particular firm. But does it follow that barring the acquisition route would result in entry *de novo*?

If a potential entrant interested in a specific industry chooses to enter by acquiring an established firm, it will have to offer a price for the firm greater than the present value of the returns expected by the sellers if they retain ownership of the firm. It will offer such a price if it believes it can manage the acquired assets more efficiently and profitably than they are being managed. There may be management efficien-

8. J. Fred Weston and S. K. Mansinghka, "Tests of the Efficiency Performance of Conglomerate Firms," *Journal of Finance*, vol. 26 (September 1971), p. 919.

9. U.S. Congress, Senate, Subcommittee on Antitrust, Monopoly, and Business Rights of the Committee on the Judiciary, *Hearings on Mergers and Economic Concentration*, 96th Congress, 1st session, 1979, serial no. 96–2, pt. 1, pp. 461–63, statement of Michael Gort (hereafter *1979 S. 600 Hearings*).

cies as a result of integration or possibilities of pursuing overlooked or neglected opportunities. Alternatively, the acquiring firm finds it cheaper to enter the industry in this way than by building new assets, a new organization, and a new set of business connections, acquiring know-how, and seeking to replicate the locational and resource advantages of the existing firm. If management efficiencies are possible and such acquisitions are barred, improvements in efficiency are thereby barred. If cheap entry is the reason for the acquisition, blockage of acquisitions may block entry. More expensive methods of entry may mean that the industry will not be worth entering. Jesse Markham found, in his extensive survey of acquiring firms, that the acquiring "companies seldom regard entry by new investment as a feasible alternative to entry by acquisition in particular industries."[10]

In either case, prohibiting *a firm that might be a potential entrant* from entering by acquisition is likely to block the expansion of capacity that would be undertaken by such a firm or permit the greater decline of capacity likely to occur in a poorly managed firm. Entry consists of expansion of capacity or maintenance of capacity that would otherwise contract. *It is irrelevant whether the expansion is by an acquired firm or by a firm new to an industry.* If acquisition is motivated by the opportunity to acquire poorly managed assets, an improvement of efficiency will lower long-run marginal costs and lead to greater output than would otherwise occur. If the entrant is motivated by a desire to enter the industry and is choosing the cheapest method of entry, the would-be entrant evidently sees opportunities for expansion or for improvements in profit not recognized by the acquired firm (except in some cases where owners sell for their own tax or estate reasons). It is for this reason that it is willing to offer a price exceeding the value of the firm to its owners.

The Effect of Foreclosing Acquisitions on Innovation

Where a potential entrant sees an opportunity in an industry— perhaps an opportunity to offer a new product or to apply a new technique—it may prefer acquisition of an established firm with a producing organization or established body of dealers in order to move the new product into the market or apply its new technique quickly. If it must struggle to build a viable producing and marketing organization from the ground up at the same time that it is trying to develop and establish an innovation, it will find the speed with which it can

10. Jesse Markham, *Conglomerate Enterprise and Public Policy* (Boston: Graduate School of Business Administration, Harvard University, 1973), p. 16.

move its innovation into use slowed.[11] The consequent slower growth may make the payoff too small and too distant for the investment in a new product or technique to be worth the cost. Established competitors will also have a longer time in which to develop competitive new products.

It appears that an organization growing more rapidly than 10 percent a year (as measured by asset growth) finds itself faced with problems that increase costs markedly. This limits the rate of entry (expansion of capacity) and confines the entrant *de novo* with an innovation to a much lower rate of entry than if it enters by means of an acquisition. The result of foreclosing entry by acquisition could be a slower rate of adoption of innovations and less incentive to innovate.

The Effect on Entry De Novo of a Foreclosure of Acquisitions

Preventing acquisition by major firms because they are potential entrants *de novo* may reduce the number of *de novo* entrants. Barring firms from selling their assets to large firms will limit the marketability of those assets. Entrance into a field *de novo* will be diminished by this reduced marketability. The incentive for entrepreneurs to establish new firms will be reduced, and it will be more difficult to obtain financial resources. Reduced marketability of firms increases the risk to those who might provide financial resources for the establishment of such firms and reduces the prospective returns to entrepreneurs. Donald Turner points out that

> to forbid [a category of] mergers . . . would narrow . . . the category of acceptable mergers, thereby drastically weakening the market for capital assets and seriously depreciating the price entrepreneurs could get for their businesses when they wish to liquidate. Such a policy . . . might have adverse effects on entry and growth of small business.[12]

The result of the recent actions of the FTC in the proposed Lancaster Colony acquisition of Federal Glass provides a dramatic example of the losses that can be forced on a firm's stockholders and employees by forbidding the sale of a firm or a division to specific would-be acquirers. Lancaster offered $40 million for Federal Glass in 1977. The FTC acted to stop the acquisition although the Federal Company informed it that the glass division was failing and would be

11. According to Exxon, this is the reason it chose to acquire a large producer and marketer of electric motors as a way of moving what it thought would be a money-saving new technology into use.

12. Don Turner, "Conglomerate Mergers and Section 7 of the Clayton Act," *Harvard Law Review*, vol. 78, no. 7 (May 1965), p. 1326.

out of business unless Lancaster acquired and operated it. The FTC replied that the Federal Company should find a more acceptable purchaser although its investment banker had solicited offers from eighty firms with no takers. Lancaster indicated to the Federal Company that FTC opposition had cooled its interest and it withdrew its offer. On February 14, 1978, Federal Company dismissed its 1,500 glass division employees, told its customers it would no longer supply them, shut down the operation, and called in liquidators to dispose of its plant, equipment, and inventories. The FTC eliminated the competitive influence of the company's capacity in the glass tableware market in the name of maintaining competition.[13]

The fate of Federal Glass and the losses caused by the FTC's antimerger policy illustrate what led Professor Turner to conclude that decreasing the demand for companies by forbidding some class of acquisitions will decrease the birthrate and growth of companies. The usual response to a decrease in the demand for anything, of course, is a decrease in the supply. Forbidding acquisitions by a class of firms in the name of encouraging entrance *de novo*, or for any other reason, will decrease the amount of entrance *de novo*. The number of new firms founded and the number of firms supplied with additional capital to grow to middle size will decrease with the decreased demand for firms. As Commissioner Robert Pitofsky pointed out in the Pillsbury–Fox Deluxe Foods merger decision:

> Long-term competitive considerations require preservation of ease of entry and opportunity for businessmen to take entrepreneurial risks. The other side of that coin is a largely unarticulated policy, a clear corollary to the first, which would preserve exit opportunities where significant anti-competitive results do not occur. It is essential that the owners of very small businesses with slight competitive potential have some reasonable flexibility to sell out.[14]

The record of the American economy in the 1960s, the period of the "giant" conglomerate merger wave, demonstrates that we need have no fears about the top 200 corporations encompassing the whole of U.S. industry, as some alarmists would have us believe will be the consequence of allowing conglomerate mergers to go unchecked. What is notable about the actual change in the U.S. industrial structure in the 1960s, in contrast to the hypothetical fears, is that the number of corporations did not decline with the great number of mergers and

13. A. F. Ehrbar, "The Needless Death of Federal Glass," *Fortune*, vol. 100 (July 2, 1979), p. 58.

14. "FTC Permits Pillsbury Acquisition of Small Pizza Producer," FTC *News Summary* (July 6, 1979).

TABLE 10

CORPORATION, BUSINESS ENTERPRISE, AND ENTREPRENEURIAL
POPULATIONS OF THE UNITED STATES, 1945–1977
(thousands)

Year	Active Corporations, Returns Filed	Business Enterprises Operating	Individuals with Self-Employment Income
1945	454	n.a.	7,377
1950	629	7,494[a]	8,988
1955	807	9,046[a]	10,200
1960	1,141	11,172	10,518
1965	1,424	11,416	10,751
1970	1,665	12,001	11,178
1975	2,024	13,979	13,003
1977	2,241	14,740	n.a.

NOTE: n.a. = not available.
a. Does not include partnerships; figure not available.
SOURCE: Bureau of the Census, *Statistical Abstract of the United States: 1980* (1980), p. 556.

acquisitions (disappearances, in the nomenclature of the merger literature) in that period. The number actually rose from 1.1 million active
corporations in 1960 to 1.6 million in 1970 (see table 10), an increase of
more than 40 percent. There was increasing diversity in American
business during the 1960s merger wave.

Even if we confine our view to the corporations in manufacturing
and mining with over $10 million in assets, the same results emerge.
There was a roughly 40 percent increase in their number, along with
1,199 acquisitions of firms in this size class, during the decade.

The increasing number of corporations and the increasing diversity of American business are both encouraged by mergers rather than
damped by them. When mergers and acquisitions can be con-
summated with little interference, there is a marketplace for firms,
both healthy and failing, that offers owners of firms a fair price for their
equities. It is encouraging to a potential investor that, no matter what
the course of his business, he can get a fair price for it at any time,
instead of having to go through the costly and time-consuming process
of liquidating assets and paying off debts. Hence a strong market in
mergers and acquisitions acts as a stimulant to entrepreneurship, new
investment, and business innovation.

Moreover, when there is a good market for firms, those who are
trying to establish new businesses or expand their firms find capital
available and on more convenient terms than would be the case if there

were not an active market for businesses. When *potential* providers of capital know that there is an active market for firms, they are more willing to become *actual* providers. Their opportunity for gain is greater and their risk of loss less in an economy that has an active market for businesses. If a firm seeks capital to take advantage of an expanding opportunity, it will find that capital easier to obtain in these circumstances. If it grows to a size with which its current officers have little experience, the stockholders are not stuck with a management that cannot handle this problem. The firm can be sold to some corporation that has management accustomed to such a scale of operation. That makes capital easier to obtain than if there were a less active market for companies. Because a sellout is possible, potential stockholders and lenders know that they will be able to bail out of an investment that turns sour because of managerial error. The possibility of profiting more quickly in the early development of a product, technology, or market, once its promise is demonstrated, makes investment in innovating activities more attractive. If this route were not open and active, there would be greater reluctance to invest in such companies. These firms would find it difficult to grow, and the rate of increase in the number of corporations and in the number of middle-size firms would decline.

Conclusion

When Senator Metzenbaum claimed that the growth of conglomerate mergers was accompanied by "the disappearance of independent firms and the steady increase in control by fewer and fewer firms,"[15] he simply disregarded history. During the rising merger wave in the 1960s, the number of firms continually increased. "Fewer and fewer firms" was not the direction of the trend in the number of nonfarm businesses.

The claim that aggregate concentration is increasing as a consequence of conglomerate mergers is equally specious. The usual trend figures cited are those for the share of 200 leading corporations in a sector of the economy whose share is itself shrinking and in which, therefore, aggregate concentration could be expected to increase. Aggregating all nonfinancial corporations shows a very different trend in the share of leading corporations. But whatever the trend, conglomerate mergers have had such an insignificant influence on aggregate concentration that the effect is hardly detectable. All the mergers of the 1960s do not add to the equal of one IBM, and all those mergers were not with the leading 200.

15. *1979 S. 600 Hearings*, p. 8, opening statement of Senator Metzenbaum.

And the evidence that conglomerate mergers are anticompetitive does not exist. To *suppose* that conglomerates might engage in predatory pricing, reciprocal dealing, or mutual forbearance is not evidence.

The argument that the number of potential entrants into an industry is reduced or the threat of potential entry removed when a large firm acquires another outside its own field with a consequent lessening of the discipline imposed by possible entry disregards the common experience that any attractive investment opportunity has always been a *magnet* for many entrepreneurs. If anything, "the buildups in potential competition implicit in the growth of the free-ranging multi-product firm would appear to have pro-competitive effects of a general scope and importance completely offscale in relation to the rather finicky case made for the anti-competitive effects of particular conglomerate mergers."[16] An antiacquisition policy would serve only to protect slothful managment of existing firms either from a takeover or from entry and competition by a newcomer who is likely to disregard any anticompetitive folkways of the trade.

16. L. Earle Birdzell, "The Conglomerates: A Neighbor's View," *St. John's Law Review*, vol. 44 (Spring 1970), pp. 306–8.

6

Aggregate Concentration:
A Phenomenon in Search of
Significance

Adolf Berle and Gardiner Means, in their 1932 book *The Modern Corporation and Private Property*, first gave us the number 200 designating the group of leading corporations that would engulf the wealth of the nation. They told us that the 200 were "growing between two and three times as fast as all other non-financial corporations." They added that it would take only to 1969, at the 1909–1929 growth rate of the 200, "for all corporate activity and practically all industrial activity to be absorbed by 200 giant companies." Berle and Means described this century as a period in which "American industrial property, through the corporate device, was being thrown into a collective hopper wherein the individual owner was steadily being lost in the creation of a series of huge industrial oligarchies."[1] With the economic concerns of that day, more copies of the book were sold than of the ghost stories of Washington Irving. It went through ten printings by 1936.

The threat of a takeover by the 200 periodically resurfaces in congressional hearings, in speeches by attorneys general, and in studies by government agencies and commissions of "megacorporations" and aggregate concentration. Aggregate concentration, as used in many recent discussions, refers to the share of total manufactured *output* produced by leading manufacturing companies or the share of the nation's manufacturing *assets* owned by its leading manufacturing corporations. Less frequently, these days, it refers to the share of all nonfinancial corporate assets owned by leading non-

---

1. Adolf Berle, Jr., and Gardiner C. Means, *The Modern Corporation and Private Property* (New York: Macmillan, 1932), pp. v, 40. Berle was not alarmed at the trend. He wrote in his preface that "this development seemed in many ways a thoroughly logical and intelligent trend." He did add, "Equally, it seemed fraught with dangers as well as with advantages." Ibid., p. v.

TABLE 11

SHARES HELD BY LEADING NONFINANCIAL CORPORATIONS
OF ALL NONFINANCIAL CORPORATE ASSETS
(percent)

Year	Leading 50 Corporations	Leading 200 Corporations
1929	n.a.	49.4
1933	n.a.	57.0
1958	24.4	41.1
1967	24.5	41.2
1975	23.3	39.5

NOTE: n.a. = not available.
SOURCES: National Resources Committee, *Structure of the American Economy*, p. 290; and
1979 S. 600 Hearings, statement of William S. Comanor.

financial corporations. When the declining trend in the 200's share of all nonfinancial corporate assets became well established (see table 11), this aggregation was dropped from the debate, and attention was directed to the manufacturing sector.

Typically the data focus on the top 50 or 100 or 200 firms. The choice of the number of corporations to aggregate is arbitrary. There is no accusation of any specific number acting collusively or even of similar interests among the top 50 or 100. But the intimation is that there is something sinister about 50 or 100 firms turning out a sizable share of the country's product.

Occasional discussions also crop up of "interests." The Rockefeller or Mellon "interests" are alleged to wield enormous power over the economy through their investments in half a dozen among several hundred large corporations. At other times attention is paid to corporate directors who sit on more than one board.[2]

Concern about these issues is expressed for the most part on what must be termed ideological grounds. Economic analysis offers no case against the growth of aggregate concentration either in manufacturing or in all nonfinancial corporate activity. Few legislative initiatives have been directed against aggregate concentration. The Utility Holding Company Act of 1935 is a major exception. In a recent interview, however, John Shenefield, then chief of the Antitrust Division, recommended legislation to block the acquisition of any other firm by a

2. U.S. National Resources Committee, *The Structure of the American Economy* (June 1939), pt. 1, pp. 298–317.

company with $2 billion or more of sales or assets. His reason: "From the late 1940s until the early 1970s the fraction of manufacturing assets controlled by the 200 largest companies increased from 46 percent to more than 60 percent. We would not want to see the trend continue."[3]

This approach departs radically from our tradition of judging mergers by their effect on competition and on efficiency in the use of resources. Occasionally measures of aggregate concentration have been interpreted as indexes of "concentration of economic power." But as Carl Kaysen pointed out in congressional testimony, such an interpretation

> draws its validity from the association of overall measures with measures of concentration in particular markets, and cannot be given significance as an indicator of the distribution of economic power without consideration of concentration in particular markets.
>
> "Concentration of economic power" indicates some notion of a disproportionate distribution of influence on economic decisions. If [aggregate] concentration . . . is to be a measure of this, there must be a direct connection between the size of a firm or group of firms in relation to the whole economy . . . and the range and consequence of its . . . choices. Consideration of what determines the range of choice over which a firm excercises decisionmaking power shows that there is no such direct relation. The degree of competition in a *market* [limits] . . . the range of a firm's economic choice.
>
> . . . Some fairly high degree of [market] concentration is a necessary condition for a significant and persistent departure of a market from competitive behavior; it is not a sufficient condition, however, and markets characterized by the dominance in a statistical sense of a few large firms in terms of market share may behave competitively.[4]

Is Aggregate Concentration Increasing?

Whether rising aggregate concentration portends evil or good is an open question. But there is doubt whether such a trend exists. William Comanor, chief of the Bureau of Economics of the Federal Trade Commission, testifying in 1979, reported that

in 1958, the 50 largest nonfinancial corporations controlled

3. Edward Cowan, "Law for Size Limits on Mergers Sought," *New York Times*, December 30, 1978.

4. U.S. Congress, Senate, Subcommittee on Antitrust and Monopoly of the Committee on the Judiciary, *Economic Concentration, Part 2, Mergers and Other Factors Affecting Industry Concentration*, 89th Congress, 1st session, 1965, pp. 541–43, statement of Dr. Carl Kaysen (emphasis added).

approximately 24.4 percent of all nonfinancial corporate assets; this figure declined slighty to 23.4 percent in 1972 and 23.3 percent by 1975 . . . . Similar results appear for the aggregate concentration ratios of the top 200 firms. Concentration declined from 41.1 percent in 1958 to 39.9 percent in 1972 and 39.5 percent in 1975.

. . . The 50 largest nonfinancial corporations accounted for 46.2 percent of corporate after-tax profits in 1958, 36.5 percent in 1972 and 24 percent in 1975. For the 200 largest firms, the corresponding ratios were 73.9 percent in 1958, 55.8 percent in 1972 and 39.2 percent in 1975.[5]

Berle and Means reported that "200 big companies [in 1929] controlled 49.2 percent or nearly half of all non-banking corporate wealth."[6] It would appear from these numbers that Shenefield had his trend on backward (see table 11). Shenefield, however, referred to corporate manufacturing assets, which are only a quarter of all corporate assets, not to the larger group of nonfinancial corporations, which include merchandising, utility, mining, construction, and services corporations as well as manufacturing. Since manufacturing is declining in its share of the economy (from 33 percent in 1956 to 24 percent in 1980), we would expect its leading corporations to show a rising share of manufacturing.

In any case, assets are an inappropriate measure of ability to make discretionary decisions about prices, quality of a product, or wage rates. Share of sales or production of a specific product in the hands of the leading two to four firms has been regarded by economists as a far more appropriate measure, and many of them are becoming doubtful about the usefulness of even that measure.

Bureau of the Census data on domestic manufacturing production show a *decline* in the share of the 50 largest manufacturing corporations from 28 percent in 1937 to 25 percent in 1977 (see table 12). The 200 largest show a rise from 41 percent in 1937 to 45 percent in 1977. The fact that the shipments share of the 50 largest firms declined while that of the 200 rose manifests increasing equality of size. This, if size has any significance, reduced the power of the largest firms.

We should also take account of the fact that U.S. manufacturers compete with foreign producers as well as domestic rivals. Michael Gort suggests that "in view of increased imports, if we were measuring the proportion of U.S. *sales* rather than *production* of manufactured goods accounted for by the largest 200 firms, the percentage may well

5. U.S. Congress, Senate, Subcommittee on Antitrust, Monopoly, and Business Rights of the Committee on the Judiciary, *Hearings on Mergers and Economic Concentration*, 96th Congress, 1st session, 1979, serial no. 96–2, pt. 1, p. 18, statement of William S. Comanor.

6. Berle and Means, *Modern Corporation*, p. 28.

TABLE 12

SHARES OF MANUFACTURING VALUE ADDED AND SHIPMENTS OF THE LARGEST MANUFACTURING COMPANIES OF 1947 and of EACH CENSUS YEAR, 1937–1977

(percent)

| | 50 Largest Manufacturing Companies | | | 100 Largest Manufacturing Companies | | | 200 Largest Manufacturing Companies | |
| | Largest in 1947, value added | Largest in census year | | Largest in 1947, value added | Largest in census year | | Largest in census year | |
Year		Value added	Ship-ments		Value added	Ship-ments	Value added	Shipments
1937	n.a.	20[a]	28	n.a.	26[a]	34	32[a]	41
1947	17	17	23	23	23	n.a.	30	n.a.
1954	21	23	25	27	30	n.a.	37	n.a.
1958	20	23	n.a.	27	30	n.a.	38	n.a.
1963	21	25	25	28	33	34	41	42
1967	20	25	25	27	33	33	42	43
1972	17	25	24	24	33	32	43	43
1977	19	24	25	25	33	35	44	45

NOTE: n.a. = not available.

a. This is a low estimate since it is the value-added share of the largest companies *ranked by value of product shipments*.

SOURCES: Bureau of the Census, *Concentration Ratios in Manufacturing* (May 1981), tables 1 and 2, p. 9-7, and table 4, p. 9-9; *Concentration Ratios in Manufacturing Industry 1963* (1966), table 1B, p. 2; W. F. Crowder, A. G. Abramson, and E. W. Staudt, "The Product Structure of Large Corporations," in Willard L. Thorp, Walter F. Crowder et al., *The Structure of Industry*, Temporary National Economic Committee, monograph no. 27 (1941), table 1, p. 583, and 1C, p. 715; Ralph L. Nelson, *Concentration in the Manufacturing Industries of the United States* (New Haven, Conn.: Yale University Press, 1963), p. 90, n. 2; and National Resources Committee, *Structure of the American Economy*, p. 272, table III.

have declined.'"[7] In 1960 we imported goods and services equal to 4.6 percent of total production in the United States. By 1980 imports had increased to 12.1 percent of total U.S. production. Since many of these increased imports, such as automobiles, radios, calculators, typewriters, copiers, trucks, and petroleum products, are the same goods as those produced by the 200 leading manufacturers, the effect on their share of *sales* in the United States may well have been the decline suggested as a possibility by Gort.

Jesse Markham, commenting on the views that are held on aggregate concentration and on the effect of the conglomerate merger wave that crested in the late 1960s, observed:

> One of the most popular views on the American economy is that it is dominated by a relatively small number of giant corporations, and this dominance increases with each passing year—largely through merger. This view is uncritically accepted and widely disseminated by authors of the nonprofessional literature on the subject. FTC reports on mergers and industrial concentration often draw this conclusion.[8]

Even if the leading 200 industrials were actually to use 60 percent of the corporate assets employed in *domestic* manufacturing, their share of the tangible assets of the nation would be about 3 percent. Corporate manufacturing assets are approximately one-quarter of all *business* assets and one-twentieth of all material assets. The other nineteen-twentieths of *all* assets, excluding human capital (accumulated investments in education and training, whose total dwarfs all tangible assets), are held by mining and construction firms, public utilities, farmers, transportation, communication, forestry, fishery, wholesaling, retailing, and real estate firms, philanthropic institutions, governments, and individuals.[9] The assets held by the federal government (excluding military assets) amount to more than the total for the leading 200 industrials.

Some Causes of the Aggregate
Manufacturing Concentration Trend

If we aggregate the assets of the 200 leading manufacturing corporations, the resulting figure cannot be compared with all manu-

7. Michael Gort, "The Consequences of Large Conglomerate Mergers" (working paper, University of Buffalo, 1979).

8. Jesse Markham, *Conglomerate Enterprise and Public Policy* (Boston: Graduate School of Business Administration, Harvard University, 1973), p. 114.

9. U.S. Department of Commerce, Bureau of the Census, *Historical Statistics of the United States, Colonial Times to 1970* (1975).

facturing assets in the United States. An important portion of the assets of the 200 are not in the United States; it consists of investments in foreign subsidiaries. These are a larger part of the assets of leading corporations than of other manufacturers. Part of the upward trend that alarmed the former head of the Antitrust Division was the result of growing investment abroad. This did not increase the leaders' shares of domestic assets or their alleged "control" of the domestic economy.

In addition, if RCA acquires a car rental firm or General Electric acquires a mining company (a major part of whose assets are located in other countries), these are counted as a growth in manufacturing assets held by the 200 because General Electric and RCA are classified as manufacturing companies. Since 24.7 percent of the employees of the largest 200 manufacturing firms worked in nonmanufacturing establishments (mines, public warehouses, and wholesale, retail, and service establishments) in 1963, it is probable that over 20 percent of their assets were outside the manufacturing industries.[10] General Telephone and Electronics, classed by the FTC as a manufacturing corporation in its compilation of the assets of the leading 200 manufacturers, had $5 billion of assets in the telephone industry. GATX, also classed as a manufacturing corporation among the leading 200 corporations by the FTC, had assets consisting largely of railroad cars, which it leased to the railroad industry. It also owned a bank. Its manufacturing assets would not place it among the top 200 firms.[11]

If *nonmanufacturing* and *foreign* assets of all firms were stripped from the data on corporate manufacturing assets and a fraction with a consistent numerator and denominator computed, the proportion of domestic manufacturing assets held by the largest corporations would look very different. Scherer calculated that the largest 100 manufacturing firms had 36 percent of domestic manufacturing assets in 1963.[12] The FTC figure for that year without this correction is 46.5 percent.[13]

We get a more accurate picture of aggregate concentration trends in manufacturing by using domestically manufactured shipments of leading firms as a proportion of all domestically manufactured shipments. First, this uses consistent definitions and is not susceptible to the criticisms mentioned above. Second, leading firms are more capital

10. U.S. Department of Commerce, Bureau of the Census, *Concentration Ratios in Manufacturing Industry 1963*, pt. 2 (1967), table 24, p. 309.

11. Jules Backman, "An Analysis of the Economic Report on Corporate Mergers," in U.S. Congress, Senate, Subcommittee on Antitrust and Monopoly of the Committee on the Judiciary, *Hearings on the Conglomerate Merger Problem*, 91st Congress, 2d session, 1970, pt. 8, p. 4718.

12. Frederic M. Scherer, *Industrial Market Structure and Economic Performance* (Chicago: Rand McNally, 1970), p. 40.

13. Federal Trade Commission, *Economic Report on Corporate Mergers* (1969), p. 173.

TABLE 13

ASSETS/SALES RATIO FOR THE LARGEST AND FOR
ALL MANUFACTURING CORPORATIONS, 1947–1967

	50 Largest	100 Largest	200 Largest	All Corporations
For largest corporations in terms of assets in each year				
1947	0.88	0.86	0.82	0.60
1958	1.04	1.01	0.96	0.74
1967	1.02	0.96	0.92	0.76
For largest corporations in terms of sales in each year				
1947	0.80	0.78	0.76	0.60
1958	0.87	0.89	0.87	0.74
1967	0.89	0.93	0.89	0.76

NOTE: The figures in this table are for the 50, 100, and 200 largest manufacturing corporations ranked in terms of total assets and in terms of sales, respectively, in each specified year. Ratio in absolute terms.
SOURCE: Betty Bock and Jack Farkas, *Relative Growth of the "Largest" Manufacturing Corporations, 1947–1971* (New York: Conference Board, 1972), p. 13.

intensive than other firms, using more assets per dollar of sales or dollar of value added (see table 13). The use of asset figures overstates the relative position of the products of these firms in the nation's markets.

The shipments share of leading firms dropped from the mid-1930s to 1947, then rose from 1947 to 1954. The trend has been flat since 1954. The leading fifty firms produced 28 percent of manufactured goods in 1937, dropped to 23 percent in 1947, rose to 25 percent in 1954, and remained at that level in the twenty-three following years (table 12), although the composition of the big fifty changed considerably. The only thing alarming about this behavior of the share of manufactured output of the largest fifty firms is its *failure to rise* since the largest firms use labor more productively than smaller firms.

The share of the 100 largest industrials was the same in 1937 and 1963 and has increased by one point since 1963. The share of domestic manufacturing shipments of the 200 largest increased by one percentage point between 1937 and 1963, by another percentage point between 1963 and 1967, and by two points since 1967. *These data present a picture of trends in industrial structure that is at odds with the views presented in the 1970s by the officials of the antitrust agencies.* They are the relevant data for understanding the place of large firms in domestic manufacturing. The frequently used mixture of foreign and domestic manufacturing and nonmanufacturing assets is irrelevant and misleading.

Even the character of the data on domestic shipments must be closely analyzed to understand what any trend in shares means. Changes in the relative position of various industries occupied by leading firms, for reasons having little to do with their own activities, cause fluctuations in their share of total manufacturing activity. The automobile firms, which ranked as numbers 1, 3, 10, and 110 in 1977, occupy a cyclical industry. Since a small recession occurred in 1967, and 1972 marked only the second year of a recovery, their sales were lower in those years in relation to total sales than they were in 1977, the third year of recovery from a recession. Eighteen petroleum refiners are also among the fifty. The rise in their raw material costs stemming from the restrictive activities of the Organization of Petroleum Exporting Countries (OPEC) and the consequent rise in the prices of petroleum products caused a large rise in the revenues of these companies (but not in their relative profitability).[14] This increased the shipments share of the top fifty firms between 1972 and 1977 even as their value-added share declined. The disproportionately heavy representation of automobile, metal, and appliance firms among the top corporations has a cyclical impact on their share, and the large contingent of oil companies gives events in that industry a major influence in the measurement of shipment shares.

The trend in shares of value added for the leading 50, 100, and 200 domestic manufacturing firms shows a stronger rise from 1947, which was a low point, than the share of shipments. But value added too tends to mislead as much as to enlighten. The domestic value-added share of leading firms dropped from 1937 to 1947. It then rose strongly from 1947 to 1954. There was a much slighter rise from 1954 to 1963 and a flat trend since 1963 for the leading 50 and 100 firms. The second 100 added one percentage point to their share from 1963 to 1967 and two more from 1967 to 1977. The smaller firms among the top 200 grew faster than the larger firms.

After the 1937 to 1947 drop in leading firms' share of value added, most of the subsequent upward trend resulted from increasing fabrication of product by leading corporations (an increase in the ratio of value added to shipments), not from an increasing proportion of

14. The Citibank compilation of return on equity of more than 2,000 leading corporations shows petroleum companies earning 15.6 percent on beginning-of-year equity in 1973, compared with a 14.8 percent accounting rate of return of all leading manufacturing firms. In 1977 petroleum refiners earned 14.3 percent, compared with 15.9 percent for all leading manufacturers.

manufacturing shipments. The rise in the value-added share resulted, in part, from the ratio's rising in the thirty-five companies of 1947 that remained in the top fifty in 1954. (Their ratio of value added to shipments rose from 0.35 to 0.40.) It was also a *result of the replacement by 1954 of fifteen companies in the 1947 top fifty* by companies whose ratio of value added to shipments was much higher (0.48 versus 0.29).[15]

The rise in the ratio of value added to shipments in the largest 50, 100, and 200 industrials, which played a major role in their early increases in share of manufacturing value added, can be ascribed in part to decreasing amounts of material used per dollar's worth of product. With improving technology, fabrication increasingly replaced raw material. By this means materials were conserved. As transistors replaced vacuum tubes and integrated circuits replaced transistors and wired circuits, for example, the material required for any given output of electronic equipment dropped. The ratio of value added to the value of materials increased, as did the ratio of value added to the value of shipments. The relatively greater growth of more vertically integrated firms, which displaced some of the original top firms, also played a role in the increase in value added in relation to shipments. Assembly operations formerly fed by purchased parts began using internally produced subassemblies. Parts suppliers began using the parts they fabricated to make their own final products. Chrysler purchased Briggs Manufacturing, its supplier of bodies, and oil refiners began processing the raw materials they produced into chemicals.

This trend was simply a move toward the average degree of internal fabrication found among other firms. In 1937 the largest fifty firms produced only 20 percent of value added in all manufacturing although they shipped 28 percent of all manufactured product. They did less fabricating work on the products they shipped than the average manufacturing firm. By 1972 the largest fifty were more like other manufacturers in their vertical integration. Value-added and shipment proportions became more nearly equal. A rise in their share of value added and a *drop* in their share of product shipped (table 12) brought about the equality.

The effect of mergers on aggregate concentration has been minuscule. Professor Markham examined the trend in aggregate share between 1963 and 1970 of the largest 50 and 100 industrials. This was the period in which some emerging conglomerates, such as Ling-Temco-Voight and Gulf and Western, moved into the top 50. He concluded that, "since no increase in concentration occurred in the period of the conglomerate merger wave, the large volume of ac-

---

15. Ralph L. Nelson, *Concentration in the Manufacturing Industries of the United States* (New Haven, Conn.: Yale University Press, 1963), p. 94.

quisitions in the 1960s appears to have left the overall structure of the manufacturing economy unaltered."[16] To this, James Lorie and Paul Halpern, writing in late 1969, add the following comment:

> Between 1960 and 1968, 909 firms in manufacturing and mining acquired other firms with assets of more than $10 million. The aggregate value of the assets acquired was $40.6 billion, an amount equal to the market value of the common stock of International Business Machines Corporation on September 22, 1969.[17]

It should also be born in mind that the 50 or 100 largest industrial companies are not an unchanging group, each fixed in its position with enduring ties to the rest. Of the 50 largest manufacturing firms in 1947, only 24 remained in the top 50 in 1977. Seventeen of the 50 largest in 1977 came from outside the ranks of the 100 largest in 1947. Thirteen of the 50 largest in 1947 no longer appear among the top 100.

The reasons for such changes are straightforward. Each leading firm must work hard constantly to improve its products, keep its prices attractive, raise its productivity, adapt itself to the changing desires of American consumers, and compete effectively for labor, materials, and capital in order to stay solvent. If its major products become obsolete, it will have to change industries or join United States Leather (number 7 in 1909) or American Woolen Company (number 21 in 1909) in the corporate graveyard. The only staying power that large firms—like other firms—have is that derived from their ability to produce products at a low enough cost to offer wage rates and profits that are attractive to workers and suppliers of capital and attractive products at prices low enough to entice buyers to choose their goods rather than those of their competitors. Essentially, any member of the top fifty is there because it uses the resources it employs more productively than other companies can use those resources. If it did not, they would be bid away by other firms.

That the fifty employ people more productively than smaller firms is shown by the fact that they produced 24 percent of all value added by manufacture and 25 percent of all product shipped in 1977 with only 17 percent of the workers employed in manufacturing. The wage paid per worker in the fifty averaged 53 percent more than the wage paid in other manufacturing firms (see table 14). Those who would stop the relative growth of the largest industrials seek, in effect, to foreclose growth in the opportunity for high-wage employment. They would slow growth in productivity and speed the relative decline of the United States in the world economy.

16. Markham, *Conglomerate Enterprise*, p. 119.

17. James H. Lorie and Paul Halpern, "Conglomerates: The Rhetoric and the Evidence," *Journal of Law and Economics*, vol. 13, no. 1 (April 1970), p. 157.

TABLE 14

SHARES OF MANUFACTURING EMPLOYMENT AND EARNINGS PROVIDED BY THE LARGEST MANUFACTURING COMPANIES, 1937–1977

Year	50 Largest Manufacturing Companies			100 Largest Manufacturing Companies			200 Largest Manufacturing Companies		
	Share of worker employment in manufacturing production (percent)	Share of manufacturing payroll (percent)	Ratio of payroll per production worker in 50 largest to rest of manufacturing	Share of worker employment in manufacturing production (percent)	Share of manufacturing payroll (percent)	Ratio of payroll per production worker in 100 largest to rest of manufacturing	Share of worker employment in manufacturing production (percent)	Share of manufacturing payroll (percent)	Ratio of payroll per production worker in 200 largest to rest of manufacturing
1937	16.2	21.3	1.40	20.8	26.6	1.38	26.3	32.9	1.37
1963	17.2	21.9	1.35	23.1	28.8	1.35	28.9	35.6	1.36
1967	17.9	22.5	1.33	23.6	29.2	1.34	30.7	36.8	1.31
1972	17.9	23.6	1.42	24.0	30.5	1.39	32.5	39.6	1.36
1977	16.8	23.6	1.53	23.6	31.4	1.48	31.8	40.4	1.45

SOURCES: Bureau of the Census, *Concentration Ratios in Manufacturing* (May 1981), table 4, p. 9-9; *Concentration Ratios in Manufacturing Industry 1963* (1966), table 1B, p. 2; Crowder, Abramson, and Staudt, "The Product Structure of Large Corporations," tables 1, p. 583, and 1C, p. 715.

7

The Economic and Political "Power" of the 200

Aggregate concentration or macroconcentration cuts across individual product markets and depends on the relative size of the largest firms. It is a meaningless concept in economic terms. The fact that a firm ranks among the top 200 does not mean that it can exercise control over its product markets, nor does it mean that the firm can depress the price of some input that it uses. Exxon, for example, which produces and sells worldwide, receives 73 percent of its revenues from its production and sales abroad. It has been ranked first or second in size by assets or sales among all *American* manufacturing firms for many years; yet its place is small in the domestic petroleum products industry. It has no market power in refined petroleum products, nor can it control the prices of its raw materials. Its share of American manufacturing sales or assets is usually overstated by including its foreign sales or assets in the numerator of the ratio. It would not be at the top of the list if companies were ranked by domestic assets or revenues.

Nor is Exxon a very large firm in the U.S. market in relation to other leading oil refiners operating in the United States. It produces only 9 percent of all domestically refined petroleum products. While that makes it the leading firm in its industry, even the market-concentration doctrine would imply that such a small share leaves it without power. If it were to restrict output and attempt to raise its price in relation to costs, its position in the market would fade quickly. Any supply vacuum would be filled by the dozens of other refiners (seventeen of whom are among the fifty leading industrial firms) eager for more business and by importers of petroleum products, assuming government controls would not prevent this. If Exxon even failed to increase its productivity constantly, it would find itself unable to pay wages high enough to hold its workers or offer returns attractive enough to obtain the capital needed to maintain its position in the industry. Its power to do anything—even to produce—depends on its ability to serve consumers well at competitive prices. It moved into first place in the retail gasoline market in the United States in late 1979 only because it received crude oil from Saudi Arabia priced about five dollars per barrel below world market levels. That enabled it to offer gasoline at attractive prices and in larger amounts than other refiners could.

The Economic Power of "Dominant" Firms

The 1927 shutdown of the Ford Motor Company dramatically illustrates how little influence a "megacorporation" has even when it is large in relation to its own industry. Ford was one of the giant firms of the 1920s (and is still America's sixth largest industrial firm, though no longer first in the automobile industry). It produced 60 percent of all automobiles turned out in the United States in 1921. From 1921 to 1925 it supplied as many automobiles as all other companies combined. Ford was a "dominant" firm.

In 1927 it completely shut off its supply to the market for nearly the entire year. It closed down in January to retool for the change from the Model T to the Model A, resuming sales in December. If supplying a majority or near majority of a market gives a firm any power to control supply and price, then the complete withdrawal of that firm's supply would certainly cause a rise in price. Yet, despite Ford's "dominant" producer position, automobile prices failed to rise when Ford shut down. Other manufacturers quickly increased their output. As a result, prices not only failed to rise—they *fell* by mid-1927 despite the complete withdrawal of Ford from the new car market.[1]

The story of the American Sugar Refining Company demonstrates the inability of a firm to influence a price for long even with 98 percent of the capacity for supplying a market. American Sugar was one of the very largest industrial enterprises in the United States in the 1890s and was still the eighth largest in 1901. At the end of 1891 it encompassed by merger 98 percent of its industry's capacity east of the Rockies. Yet what power it acquired disappeared after it raised prices by 5 percent in 1892 and 1893. By 1894 it had lost one-fifth of its market (see table 5), and prices returned to their 1891 level. Similarly, American Can was a leader in size among all industrial and mining firms in 1901 and was still the twentieth largest in 1909 after losing one-third of its market share. It too found that its dominant position withered when it attempted to raise prices in relation to costs (see table 5).

If American Sugar or American Can could not long influence prices starting from positions with 98 and 90 percent of their industry's capacity, it matters little that they ranked among the fifty largest

1. Federal Trade Commission, *Report on Motor Vehicle Industry* (1939).

71

industrial firms at the time of their attempts. It matters even less that Exxon ranks first among all manufacturing firms since its market position is vastly less important in its industry than was that of Ford, American Sugar, or American Can. The fact that Chrysler was the tenth largest industrial corporation in the United States did not keep it from being a troubled company. Only the most naive observer could possibly tell its president that he controls his output, produces what he pleases, names his price, and compels his customers to buy with advertising. Such news—if it were true—would certainly be welcome at Chrysler Corporation.

Bigness and Political Power

The final argument of those who are concerned about aggregate concentration is that bigness is a threat to democracy because of the political power of the giant corporation.[2] Since there are no adequate, systematic studies of the political power possessed by "mega-corporations," we have only a few observations to report.[3]

Edward Banfield investigated business power in Chicago. He concluded that business had essentially no power "except by main force of being right."[4] Edward Epstein suggests that corporations are too reticent in the political process and should press their legitimate interests more vigorously than they do.[5]

2. U.S. Congress, Senate, Subcommittee on Antitrust, Monopoly, and Business Rights of the Committee on the Judiciary, *Hearings on Mergers and Economic Concentration*, 96th Congress, 1st session, 1979, serial no. 96–2, pt. 1, p. 17, statement of John Shenefield, and p. 61, statement of William S. Comanor (hereafter *1979 S. 600 Hearings*).

3. Lester M. Salamon and John J. Siegfried attempted such a study: "Economic Power and Political Influence: The Impact of Industry Structure on Public Policy," *American Political Science Review*, vol. 71 (September 1977). They concluded that the relationship they found between their tax avoidance rate and various independent variables "suggests an empirical base for the long-standing argument that antitrust policy is necessary to avoid not just undue concentration of economic power but also threatening concentrations of political power" (p. 1039). The conclusion is a non sequitur. Two of their five regressions (reported in a separate paper) show a positive relationship between firm size and their tax avoidance rate (their proxy for political power), but the same two regressions show an even stronger *negative* relationship between market concentration and their tax avoidance rate. This indicates that a large firm with a large market share has no political power or, if its market share is large enough, is politically repressed. If the mineral firms, in which the depletion allowance causes a high tax avoidance rate, are removed from the sample of industries, the only significant relationship remaining is a negative influence on the tax avoidance rate of a high profit rate. It appears that low-profit industries have the greatest success in avoiding taxes and high-profit industries pay disproportionately high taxes. Aside from their non sequiturs and inappropriate selection of industries, Salamon and Siegfried's study can also be criticized for its method of measuring profits and the tax avoidance rate.

4. Edward C. Banfield, *Political Influence* (New York: Free Press, 1961).

5. Edwin Epstein, *The Corporation in American Politics* (Englewood Cliffs, N.J.: Prentice-Hall, 1969).

TABLE 15

IMPORT QUOTAS OF REFINERIES AS PERCENTAGE
OF DAILY INPUT OF PETROLEUM, JULY 1, 1959–DECEMBER 31, 1959
(districts I–IV)

Size of Refinery (thousands of barrels)	Quota
0–10	11.4
10–20	10.4
20–30	9.5
30–60	8.5
60–100	7.6
100–150	6.6
150–200	5.7
200–300	4.7
300 and over	3.8

SOURCE: U.S. Congress, Senate, Select Committee on Small Business, *Hearings on Impact of System of Allocation of Crude Oil under Mandatory Oil Import Program on Small Business Refiners*, 88th Congress, 2d session, August 10–11, 1964, p. 121.

Among the ten largest industrial corporations in America are six international oil companies. If firms among the largest fifty possess any political power, then the six international oil companies in the top ten must have overwhelming "clout." Yet they were the losers from 1960 to 1973 under the mandatory oil import quota program (see table 15). They were losers again after 1973 under the oil "entitlements" and allocation programs. Douglas Bohi and Milton Russell, discussing the "interests" served by U.S. oil import policy, report:

> The major large group which *paid* for the benefits of the greater energy security achieved under oil import controls was the undifferentiated portion of the consuming public. With one possible exception, other identifiable functional groups were either unaffected, or actually made better off.
>
> The "possible exception" is the international operations of major oil companies. . . . The overall restriction on imports lowered their potential market, and its administration forced them to share the already limited market with newcomers. The special provisions further eroded their position. The sliding scale [which provided smaller refiners with special quota allocations and a relatively larger share of import "tickets"], the petrochemical quota, the Islands program, the resid program, and the overriding fact that traditional importers were required to share the quota with inland refiners all reduced the advantage of [having developed] overseas

production. Virtually every controversy was resolved against the best interests of the original major company importers, a fact with important implications when the political economy of oil is examined. The political power of oil may be great, but based on the record of the mandatory quota program, the *power is not found in the international giants of the industry.*[6]

George Stigler, generalizing from the nation's experience with regulation in many industries, concluded that

the distribution of control of the industry among the firms in the industry is changed [by regulation]. In an unregulated industry each firm's influence upon price and output is proportional to its share of industry output (at least in a simple arithmetic sense of direct capacity to change output). . . . Political decisions take account . . . of the political strength of the various firms, so small firms have larger influence than they would possess in an unregulated industry. Thus, when quotas are given to firms, the small firms will almost always receive larger quotas than cost-minimizing practices would allow. The original quotas under the oil import quota system . . . illustrate this practice [see table 15]. The smallest refiners were given a quota of 11.4 percent of their daily consumption of oil, and the percentage dropped as refinery size rose. The pattern of regressive benefits is characteristic of public controls in industries with numerous firms.[7]

Among the 200 largest industrial firms are eight pharmaceutical companies. It is enlightening to compare their political power with that of the owners of drugstores. When the Kefauver committee investigated the pricing of drugs, the pharmaceutical corporations were treated harshly. Since the prices received by pharmaceutical manufacturers are only 48 percent of the retail prices paid by consumers, it was suggested that the committee investigate the other 52 percent. Within a few hours after the investigation was contemplated, the suggestion was dropped. The force behind this was the power of the National Druggists Association and the American Pharmacists Association. They had far more political power than the eight members of the 200 club.

Richard Posner, examining special-interest legislation, concluded that large corporations have no more influence in the political process, actually probably less, than small firms:

6. Douglas R. Bohi and Milton Russell, *Limiting Oil Imports: An Economic History and Analysis* (Washington, D.C.: Brookings Institution, 1978).

7. George J. Stigler, "The Theory of Economic Regulation," *Bell Journal of Economics and Management Science*, vol. 2 (Spring 1971), p. 7.

The fact that a great deal of legislation appears to be designed to protect firms against competition . . . provides the basis for a serious criticism of our political system and, perhaps, more broadly, of the role which we allow "interest groups" to play in shaping public policy. It does not suggest a basis for a criticism of large corporations as such. The subordination of consumer to producer interests in the production of legislation seems quite independent of the size of the individual firms involved. We observe as much protective legislation in small business industries, such as agriculture, textiles, and trucking, as in large—perhaps more. We observe much protective legislation in industries where production is carried on by individuals rather than by firms—unionized trades [barbering, plumbing, pharmacy] and regulated professions such as medicine are important examples.[8]

The agricultural interests, labor unions, and environmentalists have more than held their own with the 200 in contest for political influence. The tax structure indicates a complete lack of political influence among the 200.[9] There is, for example, heavier taxation of medium and large corporations than of the very small, a depletion allowance provided for the small and medium-size oil producers but not for the majors, and double taxation of corporate earnings both as earnings and again as dividends or capital gains (the latter being largely ficticious as a result of inflation)[10] while noncorporate firms or small closely held corporations are taxed only once.

In contests with the National Highway Traffic Safety Administration, the three major automotive firms, which were among the ten largest industrial firms, and International Harvester, a major producer of trucks and twenty-seventh on the list of largest industrial companies, have lost along with their customers and the cause of highway safety. The lack of political power was demonstrated in their unsuccessful attempts to prevent the compulsory installation of antilock brakes on large trucks before they had been developed to the point where they would not be hazardous. Despite the "main force of being

8. Richard Posner, "Power in America: The Role of the Large Corporation" in J. Fred Weston, ed., *Large Corporations in a Changing Society* (New York: New York University Press, 1975), p. 99.

9. A distinction should be made between the tax rates written into tax law and the administration of tax law. There are substantial economies of scale in the maintenance of a tax relations and accounting group. As a consequence, most systematic studies find a negative relationship between the size of corporations and the effective tax rate. The negative relationship is less a consequence of political influence than the fact that it pays to hire specialists when the stakes are large but not when the stakes are small.

10. Martin Feldstein and Joel Slemrod, "How Inflation Distorts the Taxation of Capital Gains," *Harvard Business Review*, vol. 53 (September 1975), p. 99.

right," the four large truck manufacturers, which are among the top fifty industrials, did not prevail with the administration, although electronic antilock brakes had been shown to reduce highway safety. Only the subsequent slaughter, after the compulsory installation of these brakes, finally led a federal court to order the requirement cancelled.

In contrast to the impotence of the biggest of the big 200, the little firms that compose the nuts, bolts, and screws industry forced President Carter to reverse his position on tariff protection for the industry. As the *New York Times* put the matter, "the $1-billion-a-year industry...has powerful friends in Congress who protested when the President came down last February [1978] against a recommendation by the Government's International Trade Commission for protection."[11]

Earle Birdzell has provided a succinct description of the power of the 200 largest industrial corporations:

> The argument that conglomerates represent a political power threat is . . . difficult to take seriously. A large concentration of wealth undoubtedly has a substantial political capability if it can lawfully be applied to political purposes, as illustrated by the successful political use of the Rockefeller and Kennedy fortunes. The fatal problem with similar political use of corporate concentrations of wealth is that they cannot lawfully be applied to political uses, even if stockholders could be induced to agree on common political objectives and the business organization could survive the necessary diversion of effort. Salaried corporate managers are probably not as rich a potential source of political contributions as oil lessors, owners of automobile dealerships, and other entrepreneurs with substantial personal fortunes. And corporate management is rarely able to deliver the votes even of corporate stockholders, let alone employees, dealers, or suppliers. The Automobile Dealers Day-in-Court Act is eloquent testimony to the comparative poltical power of some very large corporations on the one hand and a group of "small" businessmen on the other.[12]

And we can again turn to Posner to add his observations of the political power possessed by large firms, whether large because they are the biggest in their industries and their industries are large or because they have operations in many different industries.

11. *New York Times*, December 27, 1978.

12. L. Earle Birdzell, "The Conglomerates: A Neighbor's View," *St. John's Law Review*, vol. 44 (Spring 1970), p. 314.

That the condition of being a large firm is not itself sufficient to assure protective legislation is illusrated by the embattled condition of the conglomerate corporations. These very large firms were not able to ward off highly adverse accounting [requirements] and antitrust developments. . . .

The conglomerates occupy much the same place in public rhetoric today over corporate abuse that the great monopolies of the turn of the century, such as Standard Oil, occupied in the muckraking journalism of their day. The political power of both groups proved to be weak, or at most transient. The trusts were dismembered, and the conglomerates have been buffeted from a variety of directions without obtaining any succor from the legislative branch. . . .

. . . there appears to be an abiding public need to believe in the existence of invisible, global, omnipotent, indescribably sinister forces—Satan, Freemasonry, Papism, the Jews, and now the multinational corporations. The last satisfies the traditional requirements of a Sinister Force—worldwide in scope, mysterious in its modes of exerting influence, huge and monied. The multinational corporation, and its domestic cousin the conglomerate, have enabled the critics of business and the market economy to invoke and exploit the primitive emotional needs that unite us to our ancestors whom we deride for their superstitions.[13]

Conclusion

Politicians seldom pick on labor unions—some of which exercise monopoly power on a scale undreamed of by any corporation—or on farmers. These groups possess political power that not only makes them nearly invulnerable to attack, but also enables them to manipulate the political process in ways and to an extent that would make Thomas Jefferson shudder. Yet it is large corporations that are accused of threatening any Jeffersonian character left in our democracy.[14] That they are so frequently picked as "whipping boys" by politicians demonstrates how little political power they have.

The crusade against the growth of the top 100 or 200 industrial firms and against conglomerate acquisitions is based on specious fears and a mythical trend in aggregate concentration. They provide convenient targets on which to vent anger over rising prices of petroleum products or inflation. If this were simply a harmless and entertaining

13. Posner, "Power in America," pp. 100, 103. See also Ralph K. Winter, *Government and the Corporation* (Washington, D.C.: American Enterprise Institute, 1978), pp. 58–67.

14. *1979 S. 600 Hearings*, p. 61, statement of William S. Comanor.

political game, there would be no need for concern—but it is not.

If we continue to obstruct the growth of large firms and to thwart acquisitions by large conglomerates, we will be foreclosing opportunities to workers for high-paying employment, to stockholders for rescue by acquisition from the dissipation of their assets by inept managements, and to the country for the enhanced productivity that large firms can bring about. The United States is falling behind the rest of the industrial world in its productivity growth.[15] It once led—in the period in which the growth of U.S. corporations created some of the world's largest firms.

15. John W. Kendrick, "International Comparisons of Recent Productivity Trends," in William Fellner, project director, *Essays in Contemporary Economic Problems: Demand, Productivity, and Population*, 1981–1982 ed. (Washington, D.C.: American Enterprise Institute, 1981), pp. 125–70.

8
Summing Up

The legislators who wrote our antimerger laws and supported their passage aimed at preventing restrictions on output. They did not design them to preserve the continuance or independence of inefficient firms, whether large or small. The 1890 Sherman Act outlawed "every . . . combination . . . in *restraint of trade."* Section 7 of the Clayton Act, as amended in 1950, forbade mergers "where the effect of such acquisition may be substantially to lessen competition." Lessening competition is synonymous with lessening output, since to compete less means offering less product to compete for the buyer's dollar.

In the debate on the 1950 amendment, the immediate concern was with what Congress had been told by the FTC was a rising tide of concentration. But concentration in itself was not what was feared. It was thought that high concentration, that is, a situation in which most sales of a product are made by a very small number of companies, would result in restricted output and high prices to consumers. One of the bill's supporters quoted the *Report on the Merger Movement* by the Federal Trade Commission, saying that "under competitive capitalism consumers are protected from high prices by the constant rivalry among numerous firms for a greater share of the market."[1]

Since neither conglomerate nor vertical mergers decrease the number of firms competing with one another, it would seem that it is only horizontal mergers that fall under the strictures of section 7 of the Clayton Act or section 1 of the Sherman Act. James Ferguson argues that if economies come from large size as such—economies in the purchase of advertising, of capital, and of staff functions such as legal and accounting services, all of which are inputs in the production and marketing of a variety of products—then these economies can be realized by conglomerates without increasing the market shares of individual brands of products. Allowing conglomerate mergers is a way of realizing many of the economies of scale (size), then, without decreasing the number of firms competing with one another in any

1. Representative John Byrne, *Congressional Record*, vol. 95 (1949), p. 11506.

given market.[2] It is a way of minimizing the power of a corporation without sacrificing the economies of size. We can eat our cake (of economies of scale) and have it too (low concentration in markets) by a policy of encouraging conglomerate mergers.

Should Horizontal Mergers be Restrained?

Whether conglomerate mergers should be encouraged and horizontal mergers discouraged may, however, be best left to the market. There may be some circumstances in which most economies of size can be realized by one route and other circumstances in which greater economies can be realized by the alternative route to large size. No blanket policy fits the varied circumstances of different markets, different technologies, different supplies of inputs, or differing levels and types of managerial competence.

In some markets and industries, small size may be more efficient than large size. If those markets are concentrated by mergers, they are soon deconcentrated by competition. Or if small relative size becomes more economic in a market in which large size was formerly more efficient, competition soon deconcentrates the industry. Markets remain concentrated, in the absence of governmental restrictions on entry or expansion by small firms, only if that is the structure that yields the most efficiency.[3]

But we still face the question whether a few firms dominating a market might cause high prices through a lack of sufficient competition. What is the number of firms required to maintain the competition that will yield the lowest prices to consumers? Trying to maintain too many firms in a market can cause high prices.[4] With the

2. Ferguson, "Anticompetitive Effects of the FTC's Attack on Product-Extension Mergers," *St. John's Law Review*, vol. 44 (Spring 1970), pp. 394–95.

3. See tables 4, 5, and 6. Professor Sam Peltzman found that many industries had large decreases (and increases) in concentration between 1947 and 1967. These had above average increases in productivity. "The Gains and Losses from Industrial Concentration," *Journal of Law and Economics*, vol. 20 (October 1977), p. 229. The same consequences were found to accompany large decreases (and increases) in concentration by Professor Steven Lustgarten in the 1947–1972 and 1954–1972 periods.

E. Woodrow Eckard, Jr., "Concentration Changes and Inflation: Some Evidence," *Journal of Political Economy*, vol. 89, no. 5 (October 1980), found that among industries more than 50 percent concentrated, industries that had concentration changes of more than ten percentage points either up or down in any of the three intervals 1958–1963, 1963–1967, and 1967–1972 showed price increases averaging only 89 percent of the overall price increases in each of the three periods. In all industries more than 50 pecent concentrated, price increases averaged 93 percent of the average price increase for all industries. Table 2, p. 1049.

4. Peltzman, "Gains and Losses from Industrial Concentration," found that a policy of replacing large firms with smaller firms in industries more than 50 percent concentrated in 1967 would cause costs to rise by 20 percent and prices to rise by 10 to 15 percent.

maintenance of an overlarge number of businesses in an industry, we lose the economies of scale and the benefits of markedly superior management. The number of superior management teams is small in such industries as are the benefits of innovation in cases where only a few firms in an industry constantly lead the innovation parade (which soon leads to high concentration, if the benefits are passed on).

It can be argued that these benefits will come from internal expansion even when mergers are blocked. But will internal expansion provide those benefits as rapidly? Will capital be wasted and stability be sacrificed by driving the less efficient or the less innovative or the under-optimum-scale firms into bankruptcy on the road to an efficient industrial structure when the merger path is closed by a strict anti-merger policy?

From the evidence available, it does not take many competitors to cause economies of scale or size to be passed on to buyers. The evidence also points to the fact that those industries that are highly concentrated or that become more concentrated tend to reduce costs more rapidly than those that are less concentrated. As a result, their prices rise less rapidly than those of the less concentrated. This is exemplified by the 1900–1925 experience shown in figure 2. Where major consolidations occurred, prices at first fell while those industries with no consolidations had rising prices. In the later inflationary period, prices in the former group of industries rose only half as rapidly as those in the latter.

The postwar experience exhibits a similar pattern. In the industries that were more than 50 percent concentrated, prices rose by only 93 percent of the average rise in all prices.[5] Another study shows that prices declined from 1958 to 1966 in those industries that were more than 75 percent concentrated while prices in less concentrated industries rose.[6] The bromine industry provides a dramatic example of price decline as the industry went from high concentration to very high concentration. From 1958 to 1979, prices in constant dollars fell by 60 percent as four-firm concentration rose from 80 to 95 percent.[7] To judge from these experiences and those of major consolidations that tried raising prices, such as American Sugar and American Can, where prices fell back to competitive levels and their shares fell back to 75 and 60 percent (from 98 and 90 percent) respectively, mergers that put together as much as 50 percent of an industry's capacity will not have a price-raising effect as long as there are at least two major competitors or

5. Eckard, "Concentration Changes," p. 1049.

6. Steven Lustgarten, *Industrial Concentration and Inflation* (Washington, D.C.: American Enterprise Institute, 1975), p. 26.

7. U.S. Bureau of Mines, *Mineral Facts and Problems* (1981).

open entry.[8] In the case of United Shoe Machinery, another consolidation, one minor competitor was sufficient to keep its prices competitive.[9]

Concentration, Conglomeration, and Antitrust

In the Alcoa case (1946) the Court ruled that Alcoa had violated the antitrust laws solely by virtue of its large market share and its simultaneous stimulation of demand and expansion of capacity in anticipation of the enlarged demand to maintain its position. With that precedent and the Celler-Kefauver 1950 amendment to the Clayton Act, mergers that increased concentration or that could be called the beginning of a trend toward concentration, however speculative the possibility of the trend, were condemned by the Court up to the time of the General Dynamics decision (1974). In the General Dynamics litigation, in which the government contended that the merger of the General Dynamics subsidiary United Electric Coal with the Freeman Coal Company was illegal simply on the basis that concentration was increased by the merger, the Court held that statistical data are "not conclusive indicators of anticompetitive effects." The Court went on to say that "only a further examination of the particular market—its structure, history, and probable future—can provide the appropriate setting for judging the probable anticompetitive effect of the merger."

The Court shifted ground from possibilities to reality. This should be recognized in the new guidelines now being formulated. The old guidelines assume that structure determines conduct and performance. But the reality is that conduct and performance are more

8. Yale Brozen, *The Competitive Economy: Selected Readings* (Morristown, N.J.: General Learning Press, 1975); Harold Demsetz, "Why Regulate Utilities?" *Journal of Law and Economics*, vol. 11 (April 1968); and George Stigler, "A Theory of Oligopoly," *Journal of Political Economy*, vol. 72, no. 1 (February 1974). John E. Kwoka argues that a firm with a more than 26 percent share of a market has sufficient power to raise prices, judging by the relationship of price-cost margins to market shares. "The Effect of Market Share Distribution on Industry Performance," *Review of Economics and Statistics*, vol. 61, no. 1 (February 1979), p. 101. The relationship he finds, however, is more likely the result of the cost-reducing effect of large market shares where they occur or the attainment of large market shares by firms as a result of reducing costs and passing some of the benefits on to buyers, judging by evidence that Kwoka did not take into account. But even by Kwoka's standard, the merger guidelines are far too strict for horizontal mergers, particularly where a merger would enlarge the size of whatever firm would come to occupy any rank below second place in an industry. In these terms, stopping the merger of Heileman and Schlitz prevented the beer industry from becoming more competitive. The stock market also evidently believed this to be the case. Anheuser-Busch stock made a new high for the year where it became known that the Antitrust Division would oppose the merger of Heileman and Schlitz.

9. Robert H. Bork, *The Antitrust Paradox: A Policy at War with Itself* (New York: Basic Books, 1978), pp. 181–82.

likely to determine structure and that, in the absence of governmental intervention, structure will be forced by the market in the direction dictated by efficiency. Mergers occur largely because of market pressures, because of the existence of this road to greater efficiency, and because they lead more efficiently than internal expansion to the achievement of greater efficiency. Where mergers do not result in greater efficiency, they are mistakes that are costly to the merger makers.

An examination by Bjorn Eckbo of 259 horizontal and vertical mergers in mining and manufacturing industries, of which 183 were challenged by the government, concluded that the mergers were not motivated by monopolizing intentions. The Antitrust Division and the Federal Trade Commission had simply blocked the efficient road to greater efficiency. Eckbo summarizes his findings in the following words:

> This paper tests the hypothesis that horizontal mergers generate positive abnormal returns to stockholders of the bidder and target firms because they increase the probability of successful collusion among rival producers [or achievement of market power]. Under the collusion [or market power] hypothesis, the rivals of merging firms should benefit from the merger since successful collusion [or use of market power] limits output and raises product prices. This simple proposition is tested on a large sample of horizontal mergers. . . . While we find that the antitrust law enforcement agencies systematically select relatively profitable mergers for prosecution, there is no evidence indicating that the mergers were expected to have . . . anti-competitive effects. Since the data also indicate that the enforcement agencies . . . impose costs on defendant firms, we conclude that past antitrust policy has distorted resource allocation by making some efficient mergers unprofitable.[10]

A shift in the Court's view with respect to conglomerate mergers has also occurred. The Procter and Gamble merger with Clorox was condemned on the ground that Procter and Gamble was perceived as a potential entrant de novo (and that it would carry on Clorox's business at a lower cost than Clorox could attain on its own). The Court has since added restrictions on the use of the perceived potential entrant doctrine, and it has eliminated efficiency as a basis for condemning mergers. In U.S. v. Marine Bancorporation, it said that

a market extension merger may be unlawful if the target

10. Bjorn Eckbo, "Horizontal Mergers, Collusion, and Stockholder Wealth" (working paper, Faculty of Commerce, University of British Columbia, October 1981), p. 1.

83

market is substantially concentrated, if the acquiring firm has the characteristics, capabilities, and economic incentive to render it a perceived potential *de novo* entrant, and if the acquiring firm's premerger presence on the fringe of the target market in fact tempered oligopolistic behavior on the part of existing participants in that markets.[11]

The Court's opinion in the Procter and Gamble case had accepted as fact that the liquid bleach industry was oligopolistic, in spite of the presence of 200 competitors, and had speculated that price competition was not vigorous. It had not found it necessary to determine whether Procter and Gamble's potential entry had "in fact tempered oligopolistic behavior." It simply asserted, with no evidence beyond some speculation on its part, that "it is clear that the existence of Procter at the edge of the industry exerted considerable influence on the market." Justice John M. Harlan, in his concurring opinion, disagreed with the majority's view that the "anticompetitive effects with which this product-extension merger is fraught can easily be seen." He went on to say that "assumption is no substitute for reasonable probability." And he indicated that there was no support for the proposition that there was "a reasonable probability that Procter would have entered this market on its own."

In light of the Court's shift in its tests for the legality of conglomerate mergers, the new guidelines should not suggest that such mergers will be challenged solely on the ground that a potential entrant is acquiring a firm with a share greater than 25 percent of some market or greater than 10 percent in a highly concentrated market, as the 1968 guidelines do (see appendix).

Conclusion

Mergers and acquisitions facilitate "the reallocation of resources and the adapt[ation] of firm sizes and market structures to changes in relative demands, technology, and competitive conditions."[12] Surges in merger activity are manifestations, and a consequence, of changing circumstances and vigorous competition. If competition were not vigorous, changes in technology, the relative prices of labor and capital, or rates of growth in demand would not cause some firms to expand more rapidly than others and to acquire others. Instead, each would rest comfortably in its market niche, refrain from competing, and accept its share of growth. Firms with apparently widely different

11. U.S. v. Marine Bancorporation, 418 U.S. 602 (1974).

12. John J. McGowan, "International Comparisons of Merger Activity," *Journal of Law and Economics*, vol. 14, no. 1 (April 1971), p. 233.

efficiencies would quietly coexist. "That the less efficient are able to survive [would be] an indication that competition lacks the vigor which would force them to improve or retire from the field [through merger or liquidation]."[13]

Since a high level of merger activity is a sign of robust competition and expanding opportunities, the cries of alarm with which surges in merger activity are greeted are simply perverse from the point of view of improving efficiency, spurring growth, and adapting to changing circumstances. Only to the extent that we wish to remain frozen in a tradition-bound state with all the old familiar places, businesses, and occupations forever with us and progress abolished should we adopt any policy toward mergers other than one of neutrality, neither encouraging nor discouraging them. The possibility of temporary monopoly may be a reason for scrutinizing closely horizontal mergers encompassing more than 50 percent of an industry's capacity in times when there is no excess capacity in the industry, but there is no reason at all for discouraging conglomerate or vertical mergers.

Instead of being alarmed by a high volume of mergers, we should be alarmed by the opposite. "Low merger rates may . . . be cause for concern. For lower merger activity . . . may indicate that competition lacks the vigor which would compel rapid adjustment to changing market conditions."[14]

13. Ibid., p. 241.
14. Ibid., p. 249.

Appendix
The Merger Guidelines

The Von's Grocery and Pabst cases left businesses at sea about when they could anticipate a government challenge to mergers they were considering. In such a state of judicial uncertainty, there arose a widespread desire for some sort of guidelines. In response, the Antitrust Division issued, in 1968, merger guidelines "to acquaint the business community, the legal profession, and other interested groups and individuals with the standards currently being applied by the Department of Justice in determining whether to challenge corporate acquisitions and mergers."[1] The standards laid down consisted of measures of market share based on "structuralist" doctrines (see table 16).

The department's 1968 statement laid down rules concerning three classes of mergers—horizontal, vertical, and conglomerate. In the case of horizontal mergers, the statement distinguished between "highly concentrated" and "less highly concentrated" markets. The standards for allowable mergers were stricter in highly concentrated markets than in those less concentrated. In the former, a merger of a firm selling more than 15 percent of the product in a market with one selling more than 1 percent would ordinarily be challenged, said the Department of Justice. In the latter, a merger of a firm selling 25 percent or more of a product with one selling 1 percent or more would be challenged (see table 16).

A vertical merger joining a firm supplying 10 percent or more of some input to a market with a firm purchasing more than 6 percent of the material or service supplied in that market would also be challenged, according to the guidelines. Conglomerate mergers would be challenged if the acquired firm sold more than 10 to 25 percent of the product in its market, the exact figure depending upon the acquired firm's sales rank and the level of concentration in its market (see table 16).

After the publication of the guidelines, the Supreme Court square-

1. U.S. Department of Justice, "Merger Guidelines," *Journal of Reprints for Antitrust Law and Economics*, vol. 1 (Summer 1969), pp. 181–200, at p. 181.

TABLE 16

Department of Justice Merger Guidelines, 1968

Horizontal Mergers

1. Where the share of business held by the leading four firms is 75 percent or more, a merger will ordinarily be challenged if the firms involved possess the following market shares:

Acquiring firm	Acquired firm
4 percent or more	4 percent or more
10 percent or more	2 percent or more
15 percent or more	1 percent or more

2. Where the concentration ratio is less than 75, a merger will ordinarily be challenged if the firms involved possess the following market shares:

Acquiring firm	Acquired firm
5 percent or more	5 percent or more
10 percent or more	4 percent or more
15 percent or more	3 percent or more
20 percent or more	2 percent or more
25 percent or more	1 percent or more

3. Other mergers may be challenged where the acquired firm has 2 percent or more of the market, if the acquiring firm is among the eight largest in that market and the market share of any grouping of the two to eight largest firms has increased 7 percent or more in the preceding ten years.

Vertical Mergers

1. Mergers will ordinarily be challenged where the firm supplying inputs accounts for 10 percent or more of sales in its market and the purchasing firm accounts for six percent or more of the purchases in the same market.
2. Other mergers may be challenged outside the limits above if there is a significant trend toward vertical integration by merger.

Conglomerate Mergers

1. Merger by a potential entrant into a market will ordinarily be challenged where: (a) the acquired firm has 25 percent or more of the market; (b) the acquired firm is one of the two largest in the market and the top two have 50 percent or more of the market; (c) the acquired firm is one of the four largest in a market in which the top eight have 75 percent of the market and the acquired firm at least 10 percent; (d) the acquired firm is one of the largest eight in a market where the largest eight have 75 percent or more of the market.
2. Mergers that create a significant danger of reciprocal buying will ordinarily be challenged.
3. Acquisition of a leading firm may be challenged where the acquisition may increase that firm's market power, raise barriers to entry, or produce a very large disparity in size.
4. Other conglomerate mergers that on specific analysis appear anti-competitive may be challenged.

Source: Department of Justice, "Merger Guidelines."

ly rejected the use of mechanical formulas for determining the illegality of horizontal mergers, notably in *General Dynamics* in 1974 as well as in other cases, although it had earlier leaned in that direction.[2] Several leading students of industrial organization have, in recent years, disavowed their former views favoring the use of structural tests.[3] The old thesis that structure determines conduct and performance has come under strong attack, and this paradigm has been stood on its head. The modern view has come to regard performance and conduct as more likely to determine structure than the reverse, and empirical support for this view has been accumulating.[4]

The probability that vertical mergers would or could have anti-competitive effects has been taken seriously by few economists,[5] and that conglomerate mergers would or could have such effects has never been widely believed by students of industrial organization. With the growth in the body of research on the causes and effects of industrial concentration together with work in the last decade on vertical and conglomerate mergers, as well as the changes in the Court's understanding of what types of mergers are anticompetitive and the Antitrust Division's selection of cases,[6] the merger guidelines have become obsolete.

The Antitrust Division is now engaged in reformulating its guidelines concerning mergers and section 7 of the Clayton Act. Apparently, there will be only two categories of analysis instead of the present three: horizontal mergers and other mergers. The present head of the Antitrust Division regards the 1968 vertical guidelines as "conceptually unsound from the first to the last word."[7] Other mergers will be viewed in terms of their horizontal effects. The question of their horizontal effects will turn largely on the concept of "potential entry." This will be a "more dominant consideration" than it is in the existing guideline statement.[8]

2. *Recent Proposals to Restrict Conglomerate Mergers*, Legislative Analysis, no. 25 (Washington, D.C.: American Enterprise Institute, 1981), pp. 10–13. See also Robert Nitschke, "Antitrust in the 80s" (Paper presented before Workshop 1, Conference Board, Twentieth Conference on Antitrust Issues, March 5, 1981).

3. Yale Brozen, "Second Thoughts of Deconcentration Advocates," chapter 15 in *Industrial Concentration and Public Policy* (New York: Free Press, Macmillan, forthcoming). Among those whose changes in view are discussed are Don Turner, Carl Kaysen, David Schwartzman, Henry Simons, Paul MacAvoy, William Baxter, and George Stigler.

4. See Brozen, *Industrial Concentration*.

5. See John S. McGee and Lowell R. Bassett, "Vertical Integration Revisited," *Journal of Law and Economics*, vol. 19 (April 1976), pp. 17–38.

6. Federal Trade Commission, Bureau of Economics, *The Brewing Industry* (December 1978), p. 74.

7. Richard Vilkin, "Baxter Will Rework Justice Merger Rules," *Legal Times of Washington*, May 18, 1981.

8. Ibid.

A NOTE ON THE BOOK

*The typeface used for the text of this book is
Palatino, designed by Hermann Zapf.
The type was set by
Brushwood Graphics, Ltd., of Baltimore, Maryland.
R. R. Donnelley & Sons Company of Harrisonburg, Virginia, printed
and bound the book, using paper manufactured by the
S. D. Warren Company.
The cover and format were designed by Pat Taylor,
and the figures were drawn by Hördur Karlsson.
The manuscript was edited by Gertrude Kaplan and
by Margaret Seawell of the AEI Publications staff.*

Selected AEI Publications

AEI Associates Program